The United Irishmen, Rebellion and the Act of Union, 1791–1803

The United Irishmen, Rebellion and the Act of Union, 1791–1803

John Gibney (ed.)

PEN & SWORD
HISTORY

AN IMPRINT OF PEN & SWORD BOOKS LTD.
YORKSHIRE – PHILADELPHIA

First published in Great Britain in 2018 by
Pen & Sword History
An imprint of
Pen & Sword Books Ltd
Yorkshire - Philadelphia

Copyright © History Ireland
Produced in association with History Ireland: www.historyireland.com

Hardback ISBN: 9781526736673
Paperback ISBN: 9781526751454

The right of John Gibney to be identified as editor of this work has been
asserted by him in accordance with the Copyright, Designs and Patents Act
1988.

Typeset in Ehrhardt MT 11/13.6 By SRJ Info Jnana System Pvt Ltd.

Printed and bound in the UK by TJ International Ltd.

Pen & Sword Books Ltd incorporates the Imprints of Pen & Sword Books
Archaeology, Atlas, Aviation, Battleground, Discovery, Family History,
History, Maritime, Military, Naval, Politics, Railways, Select, Transport, True
Crime, Fiction, Frontline Books, Leo Cooper, Praetorian Press, Seaforth
Publishing, Wharncliffe and White Owl.

For a complete list of Pen & Sword titles please contact

47 Churc   , England

1   A

E-n   com

Contents

Preface

The 1790s is one of the most important decades in the history of modern Ireland. The decade witnessed the birth of the modern ideology of separatist Irish republicanism, the creation of the Orange Order, and the greatest bloodletting in modern Irish history in the form of the 1798 rebellion. In the aftermath of the rebellion came the Act of Union that brought Ireland into the United Kingdom for the next 121 years, and the smaller rebellion of Robert Emmet, possibly one of the most famous – and, to later generations, inspirational – of Irish republicans. Now, in the second instalment of the collaboration between Pen and Sword and *History Ireland* magazine, some of the world's leading experts on the 1790s explore the origins, nature and aftermath of the decade from a range of perspectives: from the individuals involved and their international links, to the events of the rebellion and the responses of the government, to the manoeuvres that led to the Act of Union, this volume explore the motives, actions and legacies of the republicans, loyalists, and propagandists who shaped events that left an enduring mark on the next two centuries of Irish history.

The chapters below have all been drawn from the archives of *History Ireland* (and especially from the bicentenary editions to mark the 1798 and 1803 rebellions), and have been re-edited; with regards to illustrations, every effort has been made to contact rights holders. If we have missed any, the error will be rectified in any subsequent edition.

Contributors

Thomas Bartlett is Emeritus Professor of history at the University of Aberdeen.

Allan Blackstock is Reader in Irish History at Ulster University.

Daniel Gahan is Professor of History at the University of Evansville, Indiana.

John Gibney is a historian attached to the Royal Irish Academy's Documents on Irish Foreign Policy project.

Patrick Geoghegan is Professor of Modern History at Trinity College Dublin.

The late Adrian Hardiman was a justice of the Irish Supreme Court.

Dáire Keogh is Deputy President of Dublin City University.

Gordon Kennedy lectures in history at the Boston University Overseas Programme based in Dublin City University.

Sylvie Kleinman is Visiting Research Fellow in the Department of History, Trinity College Dublin.

Stephen McGarry is an author and historian.

Ruán O'Donnell is Senior Lecturer in History at the University of Limerick

James G. Patterson was formerly Professor of History at Centenary College, New Jersey

James Quinn is Managing Editor of the Royal Irish Academy's *Dictionary of Irish Biography*.

Jim Smyth is Emeritus Professor of history at the University of Notre Dame, Indiana.

The late A.T.Q. Stewart was Reader in History at Queen's University Belfast.

Kevin Whelan is director of the University of Notre Dame's Keough Naughton Notre Dame Centre in Dublin

Introduction

Rebellions and Union

John Gibney

Between 1791 and 1803 Ireland experienced one of the most sustained phases of official repression in its modern history, an island-wide revolt that resulted in a level of brutality and bloodletting on a scale that (thankfully) has never been repeated, narrowly avoided being invaded by the forces of revolutionary France, and was formally integrated into the United Kingdom, where it would remain until most of Ireland became independent in 1922. And the ideology that led to Irish independence was a legacy of the same era: separatist republicanism.

The catalyst for much of this upheaval was one of the most notable organisations in Irish history: the Society of United Irishmen, a pro-French radical group founded in Belfast and Dublin in the autumn of 1791 and inspired by the democratic and secular ideals of the French Revolution. The brainchild of the Belfast-born Presbyterian physician William Drennan, the United Irishmen were one of many political societies to emerge in late eighteenth-century Ireland. But a clue to their importance lay in their name, as they consisted of a broad coalition between some Anglicans, some Presbyterians, and some Catholics—all of whom had grievances of one kind or another with the way in which Ireland was governed in the last quarter of the eighteenth century.

A century previously, the victory of the forces of the Protestant William III over those of the Catholic James II had opened the door to Protestant dominance in Ireland. The Anglican landed elite (the beneficiaries and descendants of the colonists of previous centuries) were confirmed as Ireland's ruling class, ruling through the exclusively male and Protestant Irish parliament based in Dublin. The 'penal' laws of the eighteenth-century excluded Catholics and Presbyterians from political life, a situation that only began to change from the 1760s onwards, as the decline of Jacobitism and the outbreak of the American Revolution made calls for the relaxing of such restrictions more relevant (it made sense, after all, to allow Catholics into the armed forces at a time when extra resources were needed). Yet the example of the American colonists had an extra resonance in Ireland which, while nominally a distinct kingdom that shared a monarch with Britain, was subject to a degree of British political control along with trade restrictions which ensured that the grievances aired by colonists in North America echoed across the Atlantic. Irish politicians such as Henry Grattan, backed by the 'Volunteer' movement of the 1780s, had successfully extracted a degree of greater autonomy for the Irish parliament in 1782. But hopes for greater political reforms came to naught in the 1780s, and this provided a context for the creation of the United Irishmen.

Presbyterians and Catholics had been on the wrong side of the law in Ireland for decades, which had bred a whole range of grievances, but many Anglicans were of the view that Ireland was ruled by a corrupt and unrepresentative elite. All three, therefore, had a stake in arguing for reforms. The most famous member of the United Irishmen proved to be a young Anglican barrister from Dublin, Theobald Wolfe Tone who, in his *An argument on behalf of the Catholics of Ireland* (1791), summed up the essential argument that they sought to make: that political reforms could not be achieved without the backing of Ireland's Catholic majority (they made widespread use of the printed word to get their message across). France offered a model for such non-sectarian politics, but after the outbreak of war with France in 1793, the authorities could not tolerate a pro-French group such as the United Irishmen.

To avoid the prospect of Irish Catholics leaning towards their traditional French ally, the government sought to ease many of the remaining restrictions on Catholics (such as the right to bear arms, to hold some civil and military, and the limited right to vote in elections). But the authorities also sought to crack down on the United Irishmen, given their pro-French sympathies. The organisation was suppressed in 1794 but was soon reorganised into a conspiratorial revolutionary movement. They had concluded that the only way to get to their objective of a democratic and secular society was by breaking away from Britain completely and creating an independent Irish republic on the French model, which made the United Irishmen the first organisation to place Irish independence at the top of their agenda.

France was not just to provide inspiration; the hope was that it might also provide support. Wolfe Tone (who had been exiled to the United States) went to Paris seeking French assistance for a prospective United Irish rebellion, and, as described by Stephen McGarry below, in December 1796 a substantial French fleet, carrying thousands of troops, arrived in Bantry Bay in County Cork. They were unable to land due to bad weather, and soon returned to France, but their presence highlighted the danger that the United Irishmen presented. The replacement in the mid-1790s of the liberal viceroy, William Wentworth, earl of Fitzwilliam, by the more conservative Lord Camden had signalled a hardening of official attitudes, and in 1797-98 a brutal campaign of repression was extended from Ulster across the island of Ireland to root out the United Irishmen. Popular loyalism (as represented by the newly formed Orange Order, discussed by Jim Smyth below) was encouraged as an additional counterweight to their radicalism. By this time, however, the United Irishmen had forged alliances with the so-called Catholic 'Defenders'; one of the many agrarian organisations that sought to police the moral economy of eighteenth-century Ireland. This alliance swelled the numbers of Ireland's revolutionary underground, members of which began to be derisively described as "croppies" in this period, as the United Irishmen and their allies allegedly cropped their hair to emulate their French revolution counterparts.

By May 1798 the authorities had rightly concluded that a rebellion was imminent but were also registering successes against the United Irish leadership, most of whom had been arrested in Dublin in March (the colourful figure of the aristocratic Lord Edward Fitzgerald, whose military experience fighting in North America had given him a key role in formulating their military plans, was an exception). The rebellion itself was due to break out in Dublin on 23 May. It was stopped before it could begin due to swift action by the authorities, but associated risings around the edges of the city did take place, in counties Wicklow, Kildare, Meath, and north county Dublin. The focus of the rebellion, however, soon shifted elsewhere.

The 1798 rebellion lasted a matter of weeks; modern estimates of the death toll usually suggest an upper limit in the region of thirty thousand. There were three principal areas in which it took place. The initial epicentre of the rebellion became the south-eastern county of Wexford, where the uprising began with notable rebel victories, such as the captures of the towns of Wexford and Enniscorthy. Ferocious fighting took place in towns such as New Ross before a rebel force of around twenty thousand strong was defeated at Vinegar Hill outside Enniscorthy on 21 June, and the rebellion in the southeast was crushed. Wexford was the venue for some notorious sectarian atrocities carried out by members of the United Irishmen (including the massacre at Scullabogue, discussed by Daniel Gahan below). Government forces were also responsible for widespread and bloody excesses, such as the mass shooting of untried suspects at Dunlavin in County Wicklow. Yet to many observers, the killings in Wexford seemed to confirm the fears of loyalists that, regardless of the secular principles of the United Irishmen, the rebellion of 1798 was simply a sectarian war against Protestants.

Ironically, the second major focal point of the rebellion was in counties Antrim and Down, where the United Irishmen who rose up were Presbyterians rather than Catholics. This was also suppressed brutally after the United Irish forces were defeated at the battle of Ballynahinch on 12 June. There was a postscript in County Mayo in August, when a small number of French troops under Jean Joseph Humbert landed at Killala and embarked on a lightning campaign through Connacht, scoring a notable victory over British forces at Castlebar before surrendering to the Marquess of Cornwallis on 8 September. The "year of the French" (*bliain na bhFrancach*) had a long afterlife in folklore. Wolfe Tone, who now held a commission in the French Army, attempted to return to Ireland with a second French expedition in October 1798 but this was intercepted en route to County Donegal. Tone was sentenced to death as a rebel—which meant he faced hanging—after his demand to be executed by firing squad, as a prisoner of war, was dismissed (he died after attempting to cut his own throat in captivity).

The 1798 rebellion was a disaster from a British point of view, given that it had held out the prospect of the French gaining a foothold in Ireland in time of war. In their eyes it had either been provoked by heavy-handed repression by the Protestant ruling elite, or had been permitted to happen due to neglect. The British held Irish Protestants partially responsible for what had happened in 1798, and in the aftermath the prime minister, William Pitt, revived an older idea: a parliamentary union between Britain and Ireland, akin to that which had made Scotland part of a new 'United Kingdom' in 1707.

The Irish Act of Union of 1800 ended Ireland's status as a separate kingdom as it was now integrated into a newly expanded United Kingdom. The parliament in Dublin was abolished, and Irish parliamentary representatives were to sit in Westminster instead (some of them still do). The union was intended to strengthen British control over Ireland, but it was hoped that it might help to defuse the sectarian divisions that characterised Irish life; the fears of Protestants that they remained a minority in Ireland was to be offset by the fact that they would become part of a Protestant majority in the United Kingdom as whole.

The union was defeated in parliament in January 1799 (reasons for opposing it ranged from lingering patriotic sentiment to commercial concerns, to a fear that the union would threaten Protestant "ascendancy" in Ireland). A second attempt to pass the union, complete with greater incentives to vote the right way (as Patrick Geoghegan explores in his essay), succeeded in 1800. The Catholic community were kept onside by a private understanding that emancipation—the granting of the right of Catholics to sit in parliament—would follow (not, as it turned out, until 1829). On 1 January 1801 the United Kingdom of Great Britain and Ireland came into existence; the current version of the union flag was first flown in Dublin on that day. The island of Ireland would remain within the framework of the UK for the next 121 years.

The last gasp of the United Irishmen came in 1803, with the abortive rebellion carried out under the leadership of Robert Emmet (the son of the Irish state physician). As early as January 1799 the United Irishmen had begun to regroup, and in April 1799 Emmet had fled to Hamburg to avoid arrest, thence to France, where he unsuccessfully tried to get French assistance for another rebellion. He returned to Ireland in October 1802 and continued to conspire. His rebellion was intended to be a smaller but more purposeful affair, concentrated on Dublin, that would involve a much smaller band of conspirators; its course is recounted in Ruán O'Donnell's essay below. Emmet's eventual trial on 19 September 1803, involved one of the most famous speeches in Irish history, in which he assured his listeners from the dock that he would have fought the French as well if they had attempted to impose tyranny on Ireland, and famously demanded that his epitaph not be written until Ireland took its place among the independent nations of the earth (he was executed, and his final resting place is unknown).

The United Irishmen faded away after this, though many of their exiled and imprisoned members made lives and careers in Australia and the United States. Yet the events that they were involved in had a profound impact on Irish history, as figures such as Tone and Emmet, and their project to secure the creation of an independent and democratic Irish republic, became a key source of inspiration to the Irish nationalists and republicans of later generations who would seek to follow in their footsteps.

The bicentenaries of both 1798 and 1803 spurred an outpouring of new scholarship that brought social and cultural history to bear on the traditional political and military narratives of the period. The chapters that follow, all of which have been re-edited from their original publication, probe the events of the 1790s and early 1800s, some of the individuals who took part in them, and their legacies.

Chapter One

Thomas Russell, United Irishman

James Quinn

On 2 July 1790 two young men engaged in a spirited argument over the merits of the Whig party in the public gallery of the Irish House of Commons. The two were Theobald Wolfe Tone, an under-employed barrister, and Thomas Russell, an army officer on half-pay. The argument, however, was a friendly one, and the two men took an instant liking to each other. That summer Russell spent much of his time at the Tone's cottage in Irishtown, where he and Tone continued their arguments and bantering, and became firm friends. Looking back on his meeting with Russell Tone described it as:

> A circumstance which I look upon as one of the most fortunate of my life. He is a man whom I love as a brother...to an excellent understanding, he joins the purest principles and the best of hearts...He well knows how much I esteem and love him, and I think there is no sacrifice that friendship could exact that we would not with cheerfulness make for each other, to the utmost hazard of life or fortune. There cannot be imagined a more perfect harmony, I may say identity of sentiment, than exists between us; our regard for each other has never suffered a moment's relaxation from the hour of our first acquaintance, and I am sure it will continue to the end of our lives. I think the better of myself for being the object of the esteem of such a man as Russell.

It was a crucial meeting for both men. They developed an important political partnership and a friendship of moving intensity, characterised by their own rough-and-tumble banter, in-jokes and nicknames. Tone dubbed Russell 'P.P.', after the fictional character of an earnest young cleric, whose good intentions to live a pious and wholesome life were invariably frustrated by his fondness for wine and women. Tone, four years Russell's senior, often adopted the role of older brother to his younger friend, frequently harrying him with advice. It was a role he enjoyed playing: on a visit to Belfast without Russell he noted: 'Generally sulky. Want P.P. in order to advise him. Just in a humour to give advice.' But Russell was much more than a butt for Tone's jests. Tone craved his encouragement and approval, and during his long exile in France continually lamented his friend's absence.

Thomas Russell – 'a model of manly beauty' according to Mary Ann McCracken.
R.R. Madden, The United Irishmen: their life and times (11 vols, 1842-60)

Russell, born at Betsborough, near Mallow, County Cork, in 1767, was
the son of an army lieutenant, and in the early 1770s the family moved to
Dublin after Lieutenant Russell's appointment as Captain of Invalids at the
Royal Hospital, Kilmainham. Soldiering was in the Russell blood—all three
of Russell's brothers saw military service, and at the age of fifteen Thomas
sailed with his brother's regiment to India, where he was commissioned ensign
in the 100 regiment of foot in July 1783. He saw action in the Mysore wars at

Theobald Wolfe Tone – four years Russell's senior, he often adopted the role of older brother to his younger friend, frequently harrying him with advice. R.R. Madden, The United Irishmen: their life and times (11 vols, 1842-60)

High Street, Belfast – Russell was invited to join several political clubs, in which he met the town's radical Presbyterian merchants and manufacturers.

Mangalore and Cannanore and distinguished himself by carrying his wounded commanding officer from the battlefield.

He returned to Ireland about 1786, contemplated becoming a clergyman but decided against it, and spent the next four years as a half-pay officer in Dublin, living at the Royal Hospital. In September 1790, some months after his meeting with Tone, he took up a full-time ensigncy with the 64th regiment stationed in Belfast. He enjoyed the life of a young army officer in Belfast; his military duties were light and he regularly staggered home in the early hours of the morning from Belfast's taverns and brothels. A charming and strikingly handsome man, Russell was warmly received by fashionable Belfast society. A leading Belfast woman of the time, Mary Ann McCracken, described the impression he made:

> A model of manly beauty, he was one of those favoured individuals whom one cannot pass in the street without being guilty of the rudeness of staring in the face while passing, and turning round to look at the receding figure. Though more than six feet high, his majestic stature was scarcely observed owing to the exquisite symmetry of his form...The classic contour of his finely formed head, the expression of almost infantine sweetness which

McArt's Fort, Cave Hill – it was here in June 1795 that a select group – including Russell, Tone, Neilson and McCracken – swore the celebrated oath 'never to desist in our efforts until we had subverted the authority of England over our country, and asserted our independence'. (Ulster Museum)

characterised his smile, and the benevolence that beamed in his fine countenance, seemed to mark him out as one who was destined to be the ornament, grace and blessing of private life.

For his part, Russell was drawn to Belfast's liberal circles and was invited to join several political clubs, in which he met the town's radical Presbyterian merchants and manufacturers. He became involved in the preparations to found the United Irishmen, and drew Tone into the business by asking him to write the resolutions for a new society; he also played a key role in forging links with Catholic activists. He had corresponded with leading Catholics throughout 1791, and he persuaded his Presbyterian colleagues of their willingness and capacity to engage in a broadly-based campaign for political reform. Russell himself was a devout man who adhered to a non-sectarian Christianity which stressed the elements that united Christians rather than divided them; although his father was a Protestant, he was probably recently descended from Catholics, and Russell's mother may in fact have been a Catholic.

After the founding of the Belfast United Irishmen in October 1791, he participated in founding a sister society in Dublin the following month. Soon

Execution of Thomas Russell at Downpatrick Jail, October 1803. (Ulster Journal of Archaeology)

afterwards, however, he was compelled to put politics aside to earn a living. In Belfast he had gone bail for an American confidence trickster, Thomas Attwood Digges, and when the American absconded Russell was forced to sell his commission to meet the bond. After several months he accepted the offer of Viscount Northland of Tyrone, the father of an old army friend, to become seneschal (a kind of stipendiary magistrate) to the Northlands' manor court at Dungannon. But Russell's idealistic notions of justice soon collided with the harsh realities of sectarian prejudice in mid-Ulster. He was appalled by the anti-Catholicism of his fellow magistrates and possibly also of the Northland family, and he resigned in October 1792. His experience in Dungannon contributed significantly to his developing radicalism, and he never again served in any official position, or sought the patronage of his aristocratic friends.

Russell's growing disillusionment with the political status quo coincided with the outbreak of war between Britain and revolutionary France. In spring 1793 the government introduced a range of coercive legislation, creating a militia and banning volunteering and extra parliamentary conventions. Thus began in earnest the violent cycle of disaffection and state-sponsored repression that would erupt into open rebellion in 1798. Angered at the reactionary policies of the government, Russell was even more angered that the Whigs he had once so much admired now spoke of standing or falling with Britain and had meekly acquiesced in this policy of coercion. By mid-1793 Russell had shed his sympathies for the Whigs and become one of their most scathing critics, dismissing them as a 'vile, peddling, pitiful faction' and in a letter to the *Northern Star* he denounced Grattan's 'insignificant opposition' and accused him of 'declaiming, and grinning, and chattering at the abuses of that ministry, which but for him would not now exist'.

Around the middle of 1793 he returned to Belfast, where, after some months, his friends secured for him the librarianship of the Belfast Society for Promoting Knowledge (the Linen Hall Library). It was the ideal position for a man of his varied interests, which included English literature, the Irish language, biblical scholarship, anthropology, political economy, chemistry, physics, biology and geology. Before his appointment as librarian he had been engaged by the Belfast Society to collect geological samples from the Mourne Mountains, a task he had enthusiastically carried out. Russell was never happier than when tramping through the mountains, usually alone, revelling in the beauty of nature.

The position also provided the ideal cover for him to work as a United Irish organiser and to become one of the leading contributors to the *Northern Star* newspaper, writing some of its most hard-hitting articles. In 1794-95 Russell was a key figure in transforming the United Irishmen into a popular republican secret society, and he was one of the select group that included Tone, Samuel Neilson and Henry Joy McCracken which, in June 1795 on top of McArt's fort at Cave Hill overlooking Belfast, swore the celebrated oath 'never to desist in our efforts until we had subverted the authority of England over our country, and asserted our independence'. Throughout the mid-1790s he travelled widely throughout Ulster, recruiting and organising the new mass movement. There were reports of him operating throughout Antrim, Down, Tyrone, Donegal and Sligo, recruiting for the United Irishmen. In September 1795 an informer reported that 'Capt. Russell of Belfast has been appointed to the command of all the societies in the province of Ulster'; while some time later, one of the government's most reliable agents informed the Castle that the United Irishmen were ready to rise and that 'Russell...now conducts all their plans'. His role as a United Irish recruiter was commemorated in the well-known ballad 'The man from God-knows-where', in which a stranger rides into a village on a snowy night, and converses for a time with the locals, before riding out on his mysterious business.

During his travels Russell sought out the company of working people. He often discussed politics and the great events unfolding in Europe with them, shared their homes and food and came to admire their generosity and to respect their political understanding. No other prominent United Irishman proclaimed the rights of the common man as loudly, particularly in his pamphlet *A letter to the people of Ireland* (1796), the fullest exposition of his democratic outlook. In this he castigated the aristocracy for stalling progress towards reform in the 1780s, their moral corruption, their unworthiness to govern, and their useless, parasitic existence. He accused them of using their powers and privileges to frustrate the divine plan of liberty and justice for all, and contended that all men have not only the right, but indeed the duty, to concern themselves with government and politics. Only if legislation seeks to serve 'the whole family of mankind', rather than just self-interested minorities, can there be some hope that it will reflect the natural justice ordained by God.

Russell looked to a simpler, purer form of government—something akin to the withering away of the state—in which the will of a benevolent deity could operate untrammelled by greed and corruption and man could realise those rights accorded him by nature. This was his long-term hope—in the meantime he believed that it was his duty to work towards this point by seeking to achieve measures such as the complete abolition of the penal laws and a reform of parliament to make it genuinely responsive to the popular will.

But Russell was fully aware that political reform could seem irrelevant to the poor, and was adamant that it must be accompanied by radical social change. He believed that radical changes to the existing system of property-holding were required to alleviate the plight of the poor, and was aware of the many undesirable social consequences that accompanied the early stages of industrialisation. He criticised the unwholesome conditions under which people worked in the new cotton mills, and the uncaring attitude of government and aristocracy towards a poverty produced largely by their own greed. As a magistrate in Dungannon he had taken the side of local linen weavers in their disputes with their employers. While many radicals took a hostile view of tradesmen's combinations, seeing them as an obstacle to the self-regulating harmony of the market, Russell looked upon them with approval and, in an article in the *Northern Star*, encouraged their formation—among labourers and cottiers as well as tradesmen.

His feeling for the poor was more than just ideological; Russell came from a middle-class family whose fortunes were on the slide—money, or the lack of it, was a constant theme in family correspondence. When some philosophically-minded Belfast acquaintances spoke to him of the unimportance of money he is said to have exclaimed in some exasperation, 'A man must dine!' Although regarded as a gentleman on account of his bearing and military rank, Russell lived in straitened circumstances for most of his life and had a genuine empathy with the poor. Such feelings and his uncompromising radicalism earned him the respect of the more extreme democrats in Belfast, who were convinced of his readiness to take up arms. His sympathy with the poor and his pro-Catholic leanings also enabled him to make overtures to the Defenders, and he and his close friend Henry Joy McCracken were the key figures in forming the alliance between the northern United Irishmen and the Defenders.

Such activities increasingly alarmed the authorities and on 16 September 1796 they finally struck. A large military force descended on Belfast, sealed off the town, and arrested several leading United men, including Russell. Charged with high treason, Russell was held in Newgate prison, but unlike fellow United leaders was not released before 1798. During the insurrection of that year he could only chaff at his inactivity, and his revolutionary zeal was further stoked by the deaths of close friends such as Tone and McCracken. He was considerably more reluctant than most of his colleagues to come to terms with the government after the rising and even from prison was one of the chief organisers of United Irish plans for insurrection in the early part of 1799.

Packed off to the remote Fort George in Scotland by a nervous Irish government in March 1799 he was detained for another three years. His resolve, however, remained unshaken and his letters from these years reveal a determination to take up the fight again at the first available opportunity. They also reveal the extent to which millennialist views had gripped his mind. His years in prison had given him time to brood on the state of the world and increasingly he found sense and solace in biblical prophecies. The combined effect of the continuation of the war in Europe, its spread to the Middle East, and the bloody summer of 1798 in Ireland, seems to have only intensified his belief that the world was then engaged in the time of troubles which St John had foretold would precede the coming of Christ's kingdom. Around this time his political and religious views crystallised into a conviction that the Second Coming was at hand and it was his duty to prepare the way for the establishment on earth of a Christian utopia. This would be done by eliminating throughout the world the injustices being perpetrated by war-mongering monarchies which ran counter to God's will, such as the oppression of the poor, sectarian discrimination and the slave trade. He believed that the current war was 'not a contest for relative power or riches...but is a contest between the two principles of despotism and liberty, and can only terminate in the extinction of one or other, reason and religion leave one no doubt which will triumph'. When victory had been assured and the world had been made ready to receive Him, then Christ would come to earth again and rule over this earthly paradise for a thousand years—'the millennium'.

In the intensity with which he held this belief, and all his beliefs, there is much of the archetypal romantic about Russell. This was particularly evident in the depth of his passions and the emotional turmoil that characterised his personal life, notably his anguished reaction to his heavy drinking and sexual permissiveness. Prone to brooding and self-doubt, he often subjected himself to rigorous self-examination and tended to lapse into bouts of morbid despair. On his thirtieth birthday, imprisoned in Newgate, he wrote:

> To my sorrow I think I am not so good as I was a year since. I have relapsed into fornication and lust and my temper is become more irritable...and [my] swearing has increased...I will endeavour in future to avoid intoxication on any account...this will enable me likewise to guard more against women, and I hope when released from this prison to abstain from them till marriage. I will endeavour to gain a complete mastery over my passionate temper...oh Lord God Almighty...thou knowest the secrets and sorrows of my heart...it is not from thy justice, before which I stand condemned, that I expect salvation, but from thy tender mercy that I hope for pardon and forgiveness, through my lord and saviour, Jesus Christ.

Russell's personal failings were in fact something of a spur to his political career. He frequently contrasted his shame at his private behaviour with his pride in his political activism, seeing the latter as a way of compensating for his moral failings, and the only means of redemption open to such an incorrigible sinner.

After the peace of Amiens he was released in June 1802, and went to Paris where he became involved in various conspiracies with Irish republican exiles. He was finally summoned back to Ireland in spring 1803 by Robert Emmet, whom he had met soon after his release, to assist in his plans for insurrection. Emmet believed that Russell's name would be of great use in helping to raise Ulster, and he gave him the rank of general. While Emmet prepared for rebellion in Dublin Russell went north claiming that he would raise an army of 50,000 men. However, he had not set foot in the province for over six years and was sadly out of touch with the way in which opinion had changed after the crushing defeat of 1798. He rode throughout Antrim and Down exhorting the people to rise but the response he met was typified by that of a farmer from Clough, County Down, who claimed 'they would be hanged like dogs' if they took up arms. This reluctance was confirmed by news of Emmet's failure in Dublin on 23 July 1803, and the absence of any sign of a French landing. Russell had no choice but to call off his efforts and he went into hiding, but on learning of Emmet's arrest in September he made his way south to Dublin to attempt to rescue him. While Russell planned his next move, an informer notified the authorities of the presence of a suspicious stranger in an upstairs room in a house in Parliament Street, only a stone's throw from Dublin Castle. They acted immediately and Russell was arrested on 9 September. Even King George III was gratified by his arrest but, never the clearest of thinkers on Irish matters, appeared to confuse him with Emmet by remarking that his correspondence with Sarah Curran was 'curious'.

To encourage the people of Ulster in their new-found loyalty the government decided to make an example of Russell in south Down, where he had most vigorously attempted to foment insurrection. He was tried and found guilty on charges of high treason in Downpatrick. By this stage his millennialist zeal was stronger than ever, to the extent that even some of his friends questioned his sanity. When receiving communion in prison, Russell 'in the cant of the enthusiast began to speak of the kingdom of Jesus, [and] the fulfilling of the prophecies relating to the bringing home of the Jews, which he said was now commencing, that the French arms were the instruments God would use for the purpose'. In his defiant speech from the dock he recalled with pride his political activities over the past thirteen years which he said had been for the good of Ireland and the world; he described himself as a 'soldier of the Lord Jesus Christ', claimed that the world was on the verge of great changes and requested that he be given time to complete a commentary on the Book of Revelations. In denying this request the judge observed that if he was to be allowed time to make the Book of Revelations intelligible, he would live longer than most of those present in the court. Russell was hanged and beheaded at Downpatrick jail on 21 October 1803, and buried in the nearby Church of Ireland graveyard, where a simple stone slab marks his grave.

Chapter Two

Informers, informants & information: The secret history of the 1790s

Thomas Bartlett

In the 200 years that have elapsed since the 1798 Rebellion the reasons for its failure have been frequently addressed by historians. That the rebels were unable to take Dublin at the outset of the rebellion has been seen as crucial by some historians, for this deprived the rebellion of a focus and prevented the formation of some sort of representative assembly. Again, it has long been evident that the staggered outbreak of the rebellion played into the government's hands. 'We may be thankful', wrote one loyalist at the time, 'that the insurgents have acted so little in unison and have presented us with the means of beating them separately.' First the counties around Dublin had risen and been quashed; then a few days later Wexford had erupted and been sealed off; then Antrim and Down had been tamed; and finally, months later, in August–September, Mayo and Sligo and areas in Longford and Westmeath had responded to General Humbert's 'invasion', but it was by that date too late. In addition, some historians have argued that the failure of the French to intervene in large numbers in the early summer of 1798 contributed greatly to, may even have been decisive for, the rebels' defeat. No insurrection in the Atlantic world for 200 years had succeeded without substantial foreign assistance; and the fate of the Irish rebellion was to be no different. A substantial French force would have offered discipline, leadership, weaponry, recognition and perhaps an overall strategy; its absence had deprived the rebels of all of these. Finally, historians have generally agreed that Dublin Castle emerged as victor in the intelligence wars of the 1790s. Its high-placed spies, agents and informers within the ranks of the United Irishmen kept it well briefed on what they were up to and thus enabled it to take decisive counter-measures. James 'Jemmy' Hope, the Antrim weaver, United Irishman and long-time radical confided to the annalist of the United Irishmen, R.R. Madden, in the 1840s that 'we were all beset by spies and informers', and on the basis of his researches, Madden himself concluded that 'every important proceeding of the United Irishmen was known to the

George Cruikshank's depiction of the arrest of Lord Edward Fitzgerald, from W.H. Maxwell,
History of the Irish rebellion in 1798 (1845).

government'. The late nineteenth-century writer, W.J. Fitzpatrick, devoted much effort to the secret history of the 1790s and in his *Secret Service under Pitt* (1892) he agreed with Madden on the extensive nature of the Castle's intelligence sources. And yet, despite—or probably because of—this unanimity, there has been no recent appraisal of Dublin Castle's spies and agents in the 1790s: such an undertaking is therefore timely.

Even a cursary examination of the war on subversion in the 1790s turns up spectacular intelligence successes by Dublin Castle, and these have certainly contributed to its reputation for omniscience (and bequeathed to later revolutionaries a pitiless attitude towards alleged informers). The swoop on the Leinster provincial committee at Oliver Bond's house on 12 March 1798 was made possible by precise information from Thomas Reynolds, a United Irish protegé of Lord Edward Fitzgerald. Two months later, Lord Edward himself was arrested on foot of information disclosed by the Dublin barrister, Francis Magan to his 'controller', Francis Higgins (a.k.a. 'the Sham squire') who in turn passed on his hiding-place to the Castle. Throughout 1797-98, Nicholas Mageean of Saintfield kept Lord Downshire and his agent, Revd John Cleland, well informed on the deliberations of the United Irishmen in counties Down and Antrim. And perhaps most valuable of all, in October 1797, Samuel Turner

Jemmy O'Brien, Informer.

Edward John Newell was 'in the practice of going through the town of Belfast disguised in the dress of a light horseman, with his face blackened and accompanied be a guard of soldiers, pointing out certain individuals who have in consequence been immediately apprehended and put in prison'.

Caricature of the Revd John Cleland, handler of Nicholas Mageean who infiltrated the United Irishmen in Ulster. (Ulster Museum)

of Newry divulged full details of the United Irishmen's 'French connection' to the Castle: in particular, he broke the news that Theobald Wolfe Tone was in Paris, and not in the United States. Moreover, these are only the better known of the Castle's informers, informants, spies and spymasters. A trawl through the Rebellion Papers in the National Archives of Ireland will uncover many

Thomas Reynolds – betrayed the Leinster provincial committee.

lesser known, though possibly as important, agents. Captain MacNevin and Serjeant Lee of Carrickfergus kept Dublin Castle well apprised of the doings of the alleged disaffected in south Antrim. From all parts, Leonard MacNally, a.k.a. 'JW', a leading barrister for the United Irishmen, wrote regularly to the Castle advising it of the mood of the country and of the plans of his clients. For Dublin, Samuel Sproule's numerous telegrammatic letters bore witness to his tireless pursuit of information on the United Irishmen there, and so too did those of the 'Sham squire', who wrote scores of letters to Under-Secretary Edward Cooke on the goings-on of the United Irishmen and their Catholic allies in the capital. The Boyle brothers, Thomas and Edward, likewise scribbled copious notes, conveying information to the Castle about the United Irishmen in Dublin and surrounding areas. There was at least one 'Mata Hari' type of spy: Bella Martin was in government pay in Belfast (keeping an eye on disaffected Militia men), and later in County Kildare (watching the United Irishman, William Aylmer). Lastly, there were the hundreds of informations— sworn statements—collected by magistrates throughout the country which, along with the voluminous correspondence of local worthies and busybodies, when sent on to Dublin Castle, enabled it in theory to have precise knowledge of the spread and organisation of the United Irish conspiracy. In view of these varied sources of information, it is not surprising that historians have placed great weight on the efficacy of the Castle's intelligence network as a cause of the United Irish failure. Can this view be accepted without question?

In the first instance, we should note that while Dublin Castle—and the Home Office—undoubtedly had its intelligence successes in the 1790s, it certainly had its failures too. As stated above, Theobald Wolfe Tone's true residence was not discovered by Dublin Castle until late 1797, nearly two years after his arrival in Paris—and two years after his friends in Belfast had been informed of it. Again, in the mid-1790s, two of Dublin Castle's apparently well-placed informers, Edward Newell and William Bird, alias John Smith, broke cover, went public and denounced their controllers, causing huge embarrassment to Dublin Castle, and delivering to the United Irishmen a substantial propaganda victory. Newell's final letter to Camden is worth quoting: 'In return for the fifty guineas I received on Saturday I shall give you the truest information I have ever done, and one which it would be highly necessary to attend to—my Lord, the people execrate you!' In addition, despite its extensive range of informants elsewhere, Dublin Castle was poorly informed about the United Irishmen in Wexford, or else it was easily misled about the true situation there. In either case, the rising in that county in late May 1798 came as a huge shock to the Castle, all the more unwelcome because it served to re-ignite a rebellion which had shown sure signs of petering out elsewhere. In general, it might be suggested Dublin Castle relied too much on local initiatives in gathering information on subversives in the counties: it was not nearly pro-active enough in seeking out its own agents in areas where the resident gentry or magistrates were 'supine'. Finally, in the most noteworthy failure of all, a French invasion army of some 14,000 men was mobilised and a French invasion fleet of some fifty ships was assembled at Brest in western France in late 1796, without British intelligence learning of the undertaking. Moreover, as is well known, the French fleet managed to sail out of Brest, evade the blockading ships, make its way to Bantry Bay in County Cork, spend around two weeks off Bantry (and elsewhere) and then return to its home port largely unchallenged. In the gravest threat faced by the British state between the Armada of 1588 and the threatened German invasion of 1940, British (and Irish) intelligence was found wanting.

Secondly, we should be wary of accepting uncritically the judgement of nineteenth-century historians such as W.J. Fitzpatrick on the effectiveness of Castle intelligence in the 1790s. Fitzpatrick, a pious Catholic, wrote and revised most of his work on the secret history of the 1790s at the time of the Fenian conspiracy, a movement which the Catholic Church bitterly denounced. However, for those who admired the 'men of '98', the Church's condemnation of the Fenians posed something of a dilemma, for were not the Fenians avowedly following in the footsteps of the United Irishmen? One answer to this difficulty was to downplay the role of lay leaders in the 1798 rebellion and to highlight the role of the priests such as Father John Murphy: in the end, it had been the priests who had come to the rescue of their flock and taken on a leadership role; it had been the lay leaders who had abandoned, or betrayed them. The near certainty of betrayal was the central moral of Fitzpatrick's work on secret societies: 'The organisers of illegal societies will see that in spite of the apparent secrecy and ingenuity of their system, informers sit with them at the same council board and dinner table ready at any moment to sell their blood and that the wider the ramifications of conspiracy the greater becomes the certainty of detection'.

This notion was one which the Catholic Church found serviceable in its campaign to keep people out of conspiracies. For its part, the British government too found the ubiquity of informers useful, for the promise of discovery might possibly help deter recruits from joining underground conspiracies. And in any case, the alleged Irish propensity to betray one another fitted well into that clutch of negative stereotypes (along with fecklessness, improvidence, laziness, murderousness and inconstancy) that coloured British attitudes towards the Irish in the late nineteenth century. Lastly, it should be noted that secret societies themselves found the alleged presence of those in government pay within their ranks useful, for the existence of these informers offered valuable confirmation of their importance: in addition, the hunt for these renegades gave members something to do while they awaited the great day of insurrection. On all sides, then, there was a general collusion on the prevalence of informers. Once again, however, the effectiveness of such renegades has been assumed rather than demonstrated.

Thirdly, it is now well established that in intelligence work, the receipt of information, while important, is by no means the end of the matter. Information has to be properly processed before it can be considered as intelligence. The collection of data is only the first stage in a complex procedure by which information is collated, evaluated, appraised, interpreted and then disseminated to the appropriate authority—military or legal—which then targets specific areas for more information, and so on. Did Dublin Castle have such an information processing structure in the 1790s? It appears not. Edward Cooke, the under-secretary at the centre of the Castle's intelligence gathering was, in effect, a one-man agency. Throughout the months of 1797 and 1798 he was in receipt of anything from 150 to 200 letters a month and while he performed heroically at his task, undoubtedly it was very difficult to obtain a clear picture of what the United Irishmen were up to. There is some evidence that Cooke had begun to create an effective intelligence-processing structure in late 1797 and early 1798: the arrests at Oliver Bond's house and the capture of Lord Edward Fitzgerald and the Sheares' brothers can be seen as the product of just such a development. But for most of the 1790s, Dublin Castle had no clear way of distinquishing 'solid gold' information from the dross sent in by the many adventurers active in the United Irishmen, and on the fringes of that organisation. Moreover, when Cooke resigned in 1801, his 'agency' fell apart because it had relied on his presence to operate efficiently. In Cooke's absence, Dublin Castle was caught out badly at the time of Robert Emmet's attempted insurrection in June 1803.

A single letter received by the Castle in June 1795 illustrates some of the points raised. On 7 June 1795, Rowland J. O'Connor at the Stamp Office in Belfast wrote to William Sackville Hamilton, Cooke's predecessor as Under-Secretary in Dublin Castle:

> I think it my duty as well as inclination to inform your government that there is now here a Counsellor Tone pretending to go to America but that his real design is to go to France and that one Russell who formerly had been in the army and who is one of the most violent democrats on the face of the earth, is going with him. Tone has been paid the greatest compliments here and a subscription of £1,500 raised for him; Samuel Neilson, Robert and William Simms, Counsellor William Sampson, Dr Randal MacDonnell, John and William McCrackens sic and many others have private meetings with him and have often gone with him to visit different

parts of the coast and taking plans of it; if his and Russell's papers were examined, I would forfeit my existence if some useful discoveries were not made. There are now in this town sixteen different societies of United Irish and the generality of the people here wish and are very ripe for a revolution. I believe Tone will sail in 3 or 4 days. I have the honour to be etc.

In just under 200 words, O'Connor had described the future strategy of the United Irishmen and he had correctly identified the major figures within that organisation, many of whom would be active in 1798. This is one of those letters that evokes a whistle of appreciation from the historian; yet no notice whatsoever appears to have been taken of it at the time or subsequently. O'Connor's tip that Tone's ultimate destination was France was completely disregarded; and even his remark that Tone and his companions were taking plans of the coast went unremarked. For most of the 1790s, the reality was that Dublin Castle was not prepared for an intelligence war and did not possess a clear method of distinguishing misinformation or exaggeration from the real thing. Indeed it might even be suggested that as the letters from informers and informants mounted and Dublin Castle's information increased, it may be that its intelligence on the United Irishmen and their Defender allies actually diminished. The argument that the Castle's penetration of the United Irish was a key reason for the failure of their conspiracy remains to be proven.

Chapter Three

The men of no popery:
The origins of the Orange Order

Jim Smyth

We'll fight to the last in the honest old cause,

And guard our religion, our freedom and laws.

We'll fight for our country, our king and his crown,

And make all the traitors and croppies lie down.

As the television documentaries, radio programmes and newspaper features marking the bicentenary of the French revolution rolled on through 1989, no one can have been left in any doubt where the pundits stood. The revolution was no longer considered to have been a good thing. According to current orthodoxies the costs of the Terror outweighed the benefits of the Rights of Man and Citizen (which would, in any event, have been achieved without the bloodshed). These views were very different from those enshrined in the 'Great Tradition' of historiography, which celebrated the revolution for its contribution not only to the progress of French civilisation but to the world.

One consequence of the partial eclipse of the 'Great Tradition' was the increasingly fashionable study of counter-revolution. A similar trajectory was traceable in English historiography. Over forty years ago E.P. Thompson added a postscript to the paperback edition of his classic *The making of the English working class* (originally published in 1963), in which he answered the book's many critics. Rebutting his detractors with characteristic gusto, he nonetheless accepted the objection that he had paid insufficient attention to 'the flag-saluting, foreigner-hating, peer-respecting' side of the plebeian mind. Popular xenophobia, deference and loyalism, Thompson conceded, were too little examined and less understood. That was in 1968. Today the study of militant loyalism and 'vulgar conservativism' in the 1790s is a booming cottage industry.

Lurid cartoon entitled 'Peep O' Day Boys', J.B. Daly (ed.), Ireland in '98 (1888). The caption is probably inaccurate because the villains are in uniform.

Thompson's radical reformers have been overshadowed by Linda Colley's flag-saluting Britons.

Irish historians have not followed English and French trends. The foundation of the Orange Order in September 1795 has not attracted the same level of scholarly attention as the United Irishmen. This may be explained by the sheer scale of the radical movement. The United Irishmen mounted a more formidable challenge to the government than either its English or Scottish counterparts, while inversely Irish popular loyalism, mobilised by the Orange Societies, never achieved the nation-wide support enjoyed by the British 'church and king' associations. Yet the Orange Order survives to this day, it played a prominent and controversial role in the Irish counter-revolution and it offers a fascinating example of the dynamics of popular politicisation in the late eighteenth century.

Orangeism conformed to international patterns. As well as stimulating radical revivals across Europe and the British Isles, the French revolution polarised politics everywhere. In each country the revivified radical movements confronted conservative and royalist anti-'Jacobin' crusades. Sir Richard Musgrave, the loyalist historian of the rebellion, and himself an Orangeman, made the point that 'in the year 1792 when the dissemination of treason and the formation of seditious clubs in London threatened the immediate destruction of the constitution...loyal societies checked the progress and baneful effects of their doctrines. The institution of the Orangemen did not differ from them in the smallest degree'. It is true that in its devotion to the Protestant constitution, church and crown, as in its opposition to French principles, domestic 'Jacobinism', Thomas Paine and all his works, Orangeism paralleled British loyalist movements; but its roots lay deep in the Ulster countryside.

The Orange Order was forged in the crucible of sectarian conflict in County Armagh. The most densely populated county in the country, Armagh was a microcosm of late eighteenth-century Ireland. Each of the three major religious denominations were represented there in roughly equal proportions, with a Catholic majority in the poorer south, an Episcopalian majority in the north, and Presbyterians most numerous across the centre. Each confessional group had a corresponding ethnic identity, Irish-Catholic, Scots-Presbyterian and English-Episcopalian respectively, and each was present to some degree in all areas of the county. That finely balanced religious demography itself helps to account for the persistent sectarian tensions. Patterns of settlement, dating back to the seventeenth-century plantation, created 'cultural frontiers', flash points of territorial dispute and inter-communal strife. All of these elements combined in the circumstances surrounding the brutal killing of the Protestant schoolmaster, Alexander Barclay, by the Catholic Defenders at Forkhill in 1791. Part of an 'improving' project, Barclay's school taught through the medium of English and intruded into a predominantly Catholic, Irish-speaking, area.

Because of their numbers Catholics appeared more threatening to their Protestant neighbours, than in counties such as Antrim or Down where they were a clear minority. The Presbyterian farmers of Antrim and Down who later embraced the union of Protestant, Catholic and Dissenter in the United Irishmen felt safe to do so; in Armagh it was different. When the masonic lodges of Antrim, Down, Derry and Tyrone endorsed parliamentary reform in the winter of 1792-93, the Armagh masons condemned them. Reform— or innovation as they denounced it—touched the simultaneous campaign for Catholic relief too closely for comfort.

An explosive religious geography reacted upon an unstable social structure and local economy. The formation of Orange Lodge No.1. followed a violent clash between armed Protestant bands and Defenders at a cross-road hamlet, named the Diamond, near the village of Loughgall. Up to thirty Defenders were killed on 'running Monday', 21 September 1795, while none of the surviving accounts record any fatalities on the Protestant side. The 'Battle of the Diamond' ranks as one of the more bloody encounters in a sequence of disturbances between the Protestant Peep O'Day Boys and Catholic Defenders stretching back to the mid-1780s. That endemic unrest used to be explained by land hunger. Following the repeal of penal laws restricting Catholic access to landed property in 1778 and 1782, Catholic competition for leases intensified,

Lt Colonel William Blacker, (Dublin University Magazine).

driving up prices and provoking Protestant resentment. Then in 1793 the Catholic relief act enfranchised the so-called forty-shilling freeholders in the counties, thus increasing the political value of Catholic tenants to landlords. The 'land hunger' explanation of the Armagh troubles has been superseded by more sophisticated theories, which stress the destabilising effects of modernisation and the political dimensions of the Peep O' Day backlash; but many witnesses to these events linked land competition to sectarian rivalry. Rather than simply discounting the land issue as the cause of the disturbances, it needs to be integrated with newer theories as one cause among several.

In fact the economic importance of land was diminishing during this period. Late eighteenth-century Armagh experienced rapid social change generated by its thriving linen industry. Much of the linen-led commercial and manufacturing expansion of the Irish economy at this time centred on Ulster's 'linen triangle', an area comprising west County Down, north Armagh and mid Tyrone. Linen, produced for sale in the market place by piece-working, wage-earning journeymen weavers, transformed rural society. By the 1790s in some parts of the county agriculture had become an adjunct to the textile industry. Land supplemented income from spinning, weaving and bleaching rather than the reverse. Armagh, noted a contemporary observer, 'is a hotbed of cash'. Inevitably the scale and pace of modernisation loosened the deference-based social controls on which the 'natural leadership' of the gentry had traditionally rested. Apprentices and young journeymen who 'got the handling of cash' before they knew the value of it, enjoyed an independence of action absent from the forelock-tugging dependency culture of landed society.

Whereas Catholic competition in the land market allegedly drove up the price of leases, Catholic weavers competing in the labour market aroused Protestant hostility by allegedly depressing wage rates. Certainly, substantial Catholic participation in the linen boom is not in doubt. Prominent Catholic radicals, such as Luke Teeling in Lisburn and Bernard Coile in Lurgan, were wealthy linen merchants. The brother of the Armagh priest, Defender and United Irishman, James Coigly, employed up to a hundred 'hands' in the county. From the viewpoint of Protestant Ascendancy the Catholic menace included a threat to the livelihoods of Protestant weavers. During the 1780s, Peep O'Day Boys raiding Catholic homes (which were also their workplaces) in search of illegally held arms, smashed domestic looms whenever they came across them. Again, the wholesale 'wrecking' of Catholic cottages by Orangemen in the winter of 1795-96 included the destruction of looms, webs and yarn. The break-down of traditional social control lurched into sectarian economic warfare.

Rapid economic change, population pressure and religious geography combined to produce a particularly volatile situation in late eighteenth-century

Irish loyalists under siege, as depicted by George Cruikshank, from W.H. Maxwell, History of the Irish rebellion in 1798 (1845).

Armagh; the disturbances, however, had a political detonator. Under the penal laws Catholics were denied the right to bear firearms—a proscription which had symbolic and political in addition to practical significance. In an age of citizens' militias and deep distrust of standing armies, the right of the people to bear arms guaranteed their liberty and property. That at least was the theory. The Irish Volunteers, first formed in Ulster in 1778, embodied classical republican and Whig ideas of armed citizenship, public virtue and legitimate resistance to tyranny. A few years later the right to bear arms received ratification in the written constitution of the new American republic. Thus in the mid 1780s when certain Volunteer companies in Ulster, Dublin and elsewhere admitted Catholics to their ranks, they unilaterally, and illegally, admitted them to fuller citizenship. According to another report, at about the same time the Armagh grandee Lord Gosford armed local Catholics for the less exalted purpose of protecting his orchards from pilfering!

Arms raids were political. The disarming of Catholics in County Armagh amounted to a spontaneous and unilateral attempt by lower-class Protestants to reaffirm Protestant Ascendancy by re-enforcing the penal laws. The Defenders, as the name indicates, began as Catholic bands formed to defend themselves from attack. But, as the movement became proactive and politicised and spread into south Ulster and the midlands, its standard tactic of raiding gentry houses for firearms echoed the original Peep O'Day Boy campaign, and in the context of the penal laws that tactic was likewise charged with political symbolism. In part arms raids represented an assertion by lower-class Catholics to equal status under the law.

At a local level the Peep O'Day Boys tried to maintain a system of privilege built upon religious discrimination. Yet in the eighteenth century popular anti-Catholicism could be a protean, Janus-faced force. Although it fed on the sort of vulgar prejudices concerning superstition and priestcraft so deftly parodied in the writing of Wolfe Tone, and although it could degenerate into the kind of hysterical bigotry personified by Sir Richard Musgrave, it had a positive side. To republicans and Whigs, from John Milton in the 1650s to William Drennan, Volunteer and future United Irishman, in the 1780s, Catholics were justly excluded from the constitution on the grounds that toleration could not safely be extended to the intolerant, nor liberty to its enemies. Those antipathies, historically rooted in Whig myths of the 'Glorious Revolution' of 1688 and Irish Protestant folk memories of the 1641 rebellion and of their deliverance from popish tyranny by William of Orange at the Boyne in 1690, were sustained by contemporary perceptions of the despotic Catholic monarchy of France. Catholics, wrote Drennan, were 'unfit for liberty'. Alongside its popular pedigree, the 'religion, freedom and laws' celebrated by the Peep O'Day Boys' successor movement, the Orange Order, had a radical and subversive potential which troubled the men of property and the government from the start.

While some Volunteer companies recruited Catholics, others remained aggressively Protestant. The Volunteers who clashed with Defenders in Armagh in 1788, or at Rathfriland, County Down, in 1792, were denounced as little more than Peep O'Day Boys in uniform. The societies of United Irishmen, established at Belfast and Dublin in 1791, were composed of veteran Volunteers; so too were the first Orange lodges. The decisive Protestant victory at the battle of the Diamond has been attributed to superior firepower, occupation of the high ground, and even old Volunteer 'discipline'. However, the shared institutional ancestry of the Orange and United societies in volunteering and, as we shall see, Freemasonry, is not as mysterious as it might at first appear.

As a form of participation in public life the volunteering experience raised levels of political awareness, but it did not predetermine the content of politicisation. In a way the mere act of associating was in itself just as important as the politics of a particular company. It is no accident that Freemasonry underwent one of its most rapid surges of expansion during the heyday of volunteering, or that it occurred above all in the Volunteer heartlands of Ulster and Dublin. Indeed in several cases Masonic lodges and Volunteer companies merged. Lodges and companies, with their regalia and uniforms, answered largely the same social and recreational demands, and the number of associations in the north testifies to the density and richness of popular culture in Ulster. By 1804 there were forty-three recognised or 'warranted' Masonic lodges in Armagh, ninety-two in neighbouring Tyrone and fifty-six in County Down. Masonic secrecy applied only to the internal ritual and business of the craft, not to membership. For example, in October 1784 a Masonic funeral held at Loughall—the site of the original Defender-Peep O' Day Boy feud—included 1,000 Volunteers and '300 Masons in regular procession'. Unsurprisingly such a common style of association provided others, sometimes Masons themselves, with a ready-made model.

The fledgling Orange Order (and the Defenders) borrowed wholesale from Masonic practice and terminology. Orange 'lodges', 'masters', 'grand masters', 'oaths', 'signs', 'degrees', 'warrants' and 'brethren' all have a clear Masonic lineage. The ubiquity of masonry impressed contemporaries. Sketching in the background to the 'Battle of the Diamond', Musgrave alleged that 'in the year 1795, the Romanists, who assumed the name of masons, used frequently to assemble in the neighbourhood of Loughall, Charlemont, Richhill, Portadown, Lurgan... and robbed the Protestants of their arms'. On 18 September, three days before the battle, a local gentleman informed the Dublin government that 'the Protestants who call themselves Freemasons go in lodges and armed', while forty years later a witness before a parliamentary inquiry recalled that the first Orangemen had employed secrecy 'to afford protection, if they could, to those who refused to join the United Irishmen; for every act of intimidation was used, and the fondness of the people for associating together, their attachment to Freemasonry, and all those private associations, gave a particular zest to this mode of keeping them to their allegiance'. James Wilson and James Sloan, who along with 'Diamond' Dan Winter, issued the first Orange lodge warrants from Sloan's Loughall inn, were masons.

The 'fondness of the people for associating together', for joining, oath-taking and 'secret' collecting, also helps to explain the apparently baffling phenomenon of Orange and Masonic lodges defecting to the United Irishmen and vice versa. These crossovers, which can be accounted for at one level by local political pressures, intimidation and bandwaggoning, were at the very minimum facilitated by the popular 'fondness' for joining, belonging and secrecy.

Despite its militant loyalism and anti-revolutionary ideology, there are remarkable parallels between the early Orange lodges and the Defender-United Irish alliance that had emerged by 1795. Both were popular movements; both had antecedents in Freemasonry and Volunteering; both thrived in the divided, densely textured, modernising society and economy of Ulster. The first of these similarities concerned the government and its supporters most. Dan Winter was a publican and the first lodge masters included tailors, 'linen inspectors' and inn keepers. One early lodge, no.7, met in a disused lime kiln, other lodges, echoing 'hedge' or 'unwarranted' masonry, were known as 'hedgers' or 'ditchers' from their practice of assembling 'behind hedges or in dry ditches'. Later apologists rather implausibly deny any connection between the Peep O' Day Boys and the first Orangemen or, even less plausibly, between the Orangemen and the mass 'wrecking' of Catholic cottages in Armagh in the months following the Diamond; all of them, however, acknowledge the movements lower class origins. As one sympathetic, but socially 'respectable' chronicler of these years put it, Protestant farmers and linen manufacturers, all 'humble men...decided to have a system of their own creation, and to control it themselves...an organisation formed and fashioned by their own hands, in harmony with their own ideas, and outside the control of landed proprietors, agents, bailiffs, baronial constables, and all the rest'.

Predictably, that robust spirit of independence in turn excited the 'decided antagonism of some of the gentry'. Local gentry families, such as the Blackers and the Verners, were involved in the Orange Order within weeks of its formation and the men of property effected a virtual take-over within about eighteen months, a process culminating in the establishment of a Grand National Lodge boasting several peers and prominent Protestant ultras, in Dublin in 1798. Nevertheless, Orangeism began as a popular initiative. The gentry assumed leadership as a means of reasserting control over a volatile tenantry. Generals Lake and Knox grudgingly harnessed the Orangemen as a counter-insurgency force during a period of crisis. But many magistrates remained distrustful. From the outset Orangeism had a respectability problem.

The county elites and the government moved quickly to co-opt a movement, denounced by Lord Gosford as a 'lawless banditti', because it proliferated at such an astonishing rate. Some 2,000 Orangemen marched at the first 12 July commemoration at Lurgan-Portadown in 1796; estimates for the 1797 procession, reviewed by General Lake, run from 10 to 30,000. By 1798 nation-wide membership may have risen to 80,000, many of whom enrolled in the government sponsored Yeomanry. According to one official contemporary account 'the speed with which Orangeism spread proves its adaptability to the wants of loyal men in the period'. In Musgrave's view lower-class Protestants of the established church were 'actuated by an invincible attachment to their king and country'. Certainly, the totemic popular appeal of 'loyalty' and of the blessings of the 'Protestant constitution'—the 'great palladium of our liberties'—must not be underestimated. But Orangeism's greatest appeal was defensive and reactionary, the maintenance of 'Protestant Ascendancy' against the Catholic and republican challenge.

Ireland's unstable sectarian landscape accounts for both the vitality and the weakness of early Orangeism. Like Orangeism, popular loyalism in Britain proudly proclaimed its Protestant character; unlike Orangeism the British associations' Protestantism reflected the religious affiliation of the majority of their countrymen. In Ireland inter-denominational strife and the size of the Catholic 'threat' drove thousands of lower-class Protestants into the Orange ranks. However, the same sectarian arithmetic permanently limited the movement's popular base. Still, the numbers were too impressive for a government confronted by a serious revolutionary challenge to ignore. Many an Orange Yeoman saw action in 1798.

Exclusively Protestant, the Orange Order was not, in its own view, sectarian. Its brand of Protestantism and anti-Catholicism (or, strictly speaking, anti-popery) was ostensibly political. Protestantism stood for liberty. All Protestants, whatever their doctrinal opinions were welcome to join the order, although in practice Episcopalians outnumbered Presbyterians. 'Popery' stood for tyranny and a 'disloyal' allegiance to a foreign prince; Catholics *per se* were entitled to their religious beliefs. Not that that theory prevented the United Irishmen from inventing an 'Orange extermination oath', or Catholics from believing it. Nor did refugees from the Armagh 'wreckings' harbour any doubts about the violent sectarianism of the Orangemen.

The gentry take-over of the Order in 1796-97 and Orangeism's counter-revolutionary ideology seem to fit perfectly a Marxist interpretation of it as an instrument of class rule. That interpretation treats Orangeism, and sectarianism generally, as a variety of 'false consciousness', which divides the lower classes and side-tracks them from the pursuit of their 'objective' interests. General Knox, it is true, deliberately encouraged the Orangemen in their feud with the United Irishmen in Tyrone, but on balance this thesis (which not all Marxists would subscribe to anyway) is patronising and too pat. Crucially, it fails to appreciate the self-generating capacity of popular loyalism. In Musgrave's words, rallying 'round the altar and throne, which were in imminent danger [the first Orangemen] united and stood forward...unsupported by the great and powerful.' The threat which Musgrave identified came from 'croppies', democrats and levellers. But to the government the original lower-class Orangemen also represented at least a potential threat. The men of property hijacked the movement in order to contain it.

Chapter Four

An unfortunate man: James Coigly, 1761-98

Dáire Keogh

On 7 June 1798, Father James Coigly, a shadowy United Irishman from County Armagh, was hanged on Pennington Heath in Kent. On hearing this news in Paris, Theobald Wolfe Tone, no friend of priests and of this one in particular, wrote 'if ever I reach Ireland and...we establish our liberty, I will be the first to propose a monument to his memory'. Nonetheless, as we commemorate the bicentenary of the Rebellion, Coigly remains amongst the forgotten of that year and few of the period's radicals cry out so loudly for re-examination.

James Coigly, the second son of James Coigly and Louisa Donnelly, was born in the parish of Kilmore in County Armagh in August 1761. The family lived in moderate circumstances, but like other Catholic families of the region—the Teelings, Coyles, Maginnisses and McDonnells—they provided leadership, and were a reminder of earlier dispossession and a harbinger of the late eighteenth-century Catholic revival. Armagh was perhaps the most complex county in Ireland. Not alone was it the most densely populated, but its religious demography reflected the successive waves of planters and migrants which had given the county its unique character. In the south, the Gaelic, Catholic survival was most pronounced, enabling Coigly to boast that 'not one of the plundering settlers who enslaved [his] country appears on the list of [his] ancestors'. This sense of history pervades Coigly's *The life of the Rev. James Coigly and an address to the people of Ireland, as written by himself during his confinement in Maidstone Gaol* (1798); he makes extravagant claims for his family's bravery in the Confederate and Jacobite periods, while the entire text is peppered with historical allusions.

Little is known of Coigly's life prior to his ordination at Dungannon, in January 1785. It is believed that he attended the Free School at Dundalk, where he received a classical education, after which he apparently lived for a number of years with his parish priest. In the absence of seminaries, candidates for the priesthood usually served what can best be described as an apprenticeship. After this, the candidate was presented for ordination prior to his departure to

Leading Whigs, led by Charles J. Fox (left), give character evidence at the trial of Arthur O'Connor (right) in James Gillray's vicious caricature. (British Museum)

the continent to begin his theological formation, in Coigly's case the Collège des Lombards, Paris.

Coigly's arrival in Paris on 8 June 1785, marked the beginning of a turbulent stay in the French capital. Having applied unsuccessfully for a burse at the College, Coigly took the unprecedented step of initiating legal proceedings against his superior, John Baptist Walsh, claiming that the scholarship, established in 1682 for the education of students of the Maginn, Maginniss and O'Neill families, was rightfully his. This conflict was acrimonious, but it was apparently settled to Coigly's satisfaction. Yet having achieved one victory over the authorities, he launched a second appeal, this time to restore to students the right to elect their superiors. Coigly may have celebrated his continuous disputes 'in favour of the poor down-trodden subjects', but the historian of the diocese of Down and Conor marked 'this systematic insubordination' as 'but a forerunner of his sad and subsequent career, which terminated on the scaffold'.

His second crusade was cut short by the outbreak of revolution in France in the summer of 1789. Coigly remained in Paris until 12 October. By that time Louis XVI had been brought back from Versailles by the women of Paris and within the National Assembly clerical members were shouted down. On the streets of Paris this opposition was more tangible and Coigly, having 'narrowly avoided being lanternized' or hung by the crowd, decided to flee the city.

Coigly's return to Ireland coincided with the peak of the so-called 'Armagh Troubles', the one hundred or so incidents which rocked that region between 1784 and 1791. The tensions which characterised the last quarter of the eighteenth century were particularly acute in the county, reflecting national tensions in microcosm. Armagh was the premier volunteering county in Ireland. Their commander-in-chief in the county and local grandee, Lord Charlemont, while he was to the fore in the parliamentary movement, strenuously opposed political concessions to Catholics. The Armagh Volunteers were almost entirely Protestant until 1784, but some of the more politically advanced corps had begun to admit Catholics. Yet the penal laws forbade Catholics from bearing arms. In an era when the right to bear arms was the badge of citizenship, this was not simply a security precaution, but a declaration of Protestant ascendancy.

Against this background the predominantly Anglican 'Peep O'Day Boys' began their raids on Catholic homes, removing 'illegally' held arms, unilaterally enforcing the penal laws, and re-asserting Protestant ascendancy. This initiative met with a determined response from the predominantly Catholic 'Defenders'. The significant numbers of Presbyterians in the county were more inclined towards radical politics, but were also traditionally anti-Catholic. It was imperative for the Ascendancy, therefore, to prevent a nexus between Catholics and Dissenters; towards this end, the exploitation of sectarian tensions proved a most effective weapon. It is in this context that Coigly's missions of 1791-93 must be set, as he rode through Ulster attempting to forge 'an union of the Catholics and Dissenters'.

It is probable that Coigly was a member of the Defenders; he had close kinship links with many of their leaders, while the biographer of the United Irishmen, R.R. Madden, claimed that it was he who introduced Napper Tandy to the Defenders of County Louth. His early involvement with the United Irishmen is less certain but his attempt to promote 'an union of the Catholics and Dissenters' was consistent with their programme and these forays mirrored the missionary activities of Wolfe Tone, Samuel Neilson and John Keogh in centres of sectarian conflict in neighbouring County Down.

The best source for the Armagh priest remains his own *Life* and the documents relating to his trial. While these are retrospective and lacking in objectivity, they clearly reflect Coigly's immersion in the great radical enterprise of 1792. As Madden observed, 'these efforts [of 1791-3] ultimately merged into the designs of the Northern United Irishmen, and Coigly, who appears to have been known to the Belfast leaders, as a person who had great influence over the Defenders... was early sought after to promote the views of the Northern United Irishmen'.

London Corresponding Society, alarm'd [by news of the arrest of Coigley and O'Connor], Vide. Guilty Consciences by James Gillray. (British Museum)

The demise of Fitzwilliam's viceroyalty in early 1795 and with it any hope of constitutional redress raised the political temperature in Ireland. Defenderism had spread beyond Armagh and symptoms of disaffection were to be found in fourteen counties in Ulster, north Leinster and Connacht. In the summer of

1795, Dublin Castle received reports of a growing alliance between Defenders and United Irishmen: the new viceroy Camden was determined to take whatever action was needed to halt this 'government of terror'. In north Leinster and Connacht, the administration launched a ferocious military campaign under Lord Carhampton while, in Ulster, sectarian tensions were exploited in a cynical, and ultimately successful, attempt to defeat the radical challenge.

In Coigly's Armagh such exploitation was particularly effective. The political conflict which had characterised the county since the early 1780s reached its peak in September 1795 with the Peep O'Day Boy victory at the 'Battle of the Diamond' and the consequent formation of the Orange Order. While originally a lower-class initiative, the Verners, Blackers and other local gentry families quickly identified with its counter-revolutionary potential. The Order, which Coigly dismissed as 'a church and king mob', served to reassert and defend Protestant ascendancy against the United Irish and Defender challenge. Operating outside the law, this aggressive group inflicted terror upon the region. William Blacker later described how Orangemen, moved by 'a spirit of vengeance and retaliation', resolved to drive the Roman Catholics from the region: 'It is true a great proportion of these had taken an active part as Defenders and persecutors of Protestants; still there were many who were 'quiet in the land' and had taken no share in such proceedings, but revenge like love is blind'.

Estimates vary but, in the House of Commons, James Verner, referring to reports that as many as 7,000 Catholics had been driven from Ulster, cynically declared 'whatever the Roman Catholics have suffered they have brought upon themselves'. The Coiglys were victims of the persecution; their home was ransacked in one attack, which resulted in the destruction of the invaluable historical sources assembled by the priest. This was followed by an assault on his brother's home, which disrupted the linen business which had 'kept some hundred hands at work'.

At first the authorities in Dublin and London were sceptical about the Order, but in time they came to regard this lawless faction as a vital weapon in the fight against rebellion. As Thomas Knox, the military commander in mid-Ulster, put it in August 1796, 'we must to a certain degree uphold them, for with all their licentiousness, on them we must rely for the preservation of our lives and properties should critical times occur'. Criticism of the Armagh magistracy was widespread; Archbishop Troy of Dublin referred to their 'supine neglect' and 'the prejudice of the gentry'; years later, William Blacker recalled their paralysis and Charles Teeling believed the authorities were 'passive, if not favourable to those dissentions, for *divide et impera* continued to be the motto of our rulers'.

James Napper Tandy. (National Museum of Ireland)

Ulster radicals mounted a spirited legal defence of Catholic victims of Orange outrages. A central feature of this crusade was co-operation between Defenders and United Irishmen, and prominent figures like Bernard Coyle and Henry Joy McCracken worked closely together. In his *Life*, Coigly describes his efforts to prosecute William Trumball, following the murder of his neighbour Daniel Corrigan, early in 1796. He was successful, but expressed little surprise that Trumball, 'the commanding captain of the banditti', had his sentence commuted to service on the fleet.

Coigly was deeply involved in the politics of disaffection, and his prominence had increased in late 1796 in the vacuum created by the arrests of the senior United Irish leaders in Ulster—Thomas Russell, Henry Joy McCracken and Samuel Neilson. In February 1797, the informer Leonard MacNally reported that Coigly's 'political mission [lay] at Dundalk and Armagh'; not alone had he met with Richard McCormick (United Irishman and Catholic Committee activist) and other leading radicals, but the priest was supposed to have made daily visits to the state prisoners at Kilmainham. Coigly, aware that his movements were being observed, expected to be apprehended but carried on regardless.

The United Irishmen considered running Lord Edward Fitzgerald and Arthur O'Connor for Antrim and Down in the 1797 general election; in preparation they organised meetings of freeholders in Counties Armagh, Antrim and Down which called for the removal of the Castle junto. Coigly made himself 'as active...as possible' in this campaign, distributing printed notices throughout Armagh and exhorting the freeholders 'to attend to their duty'. He was in all probability the author of an anonymous pamphlet, *A view of the present state of Ireland with an account of the origin and progress of the disturbances in that country* (1797), which Jemmy Hope believed 'contained more truth than all the volumes I have seen written on the events of 1797 and 1798'.

In his *Life*, Coigly attributed his decision to leave Ireland in June 1797 to the persecution of his enemies. In fact it was to do with divisions in the United Irish leadership, sharpened by the failure of the Bantry Bay expedition in December 1796 and the increasing pressure of government counter-measures. While the dominant moderate faction was determined to await French assistance before staging an Irish rebellion, Coigly took the radical view of O'Connor, Fitzgerald and Neilson, that independent action was essential.

Frustrated by the inactivity of the moderates and in fear of arrest, Coigly, Arthur MacMahon, Samuel Turner and others left for England in June 1797. This exodus strengthened existing links between the United Irishmen and British radical societies and these groups were to play a significant part in attempts to attract French military assistance. Coigly was ideally placed

<hr>

THE

L I F E

OF

THE REV. JAMES COIGLY,

AS WRITTEN

BY HIMSELF.

<hr>

Maidſtone Gaol, 30th April, 1798.

MY DEAR FRIEND!

HAPPY am I, even in my preſent melancholy ſitua-tion, to have it in my power ſtill to call you by that endear-ing name! My health declines ſo rapidly, that I reſolved to write you a few lines before the approach of that awful exit, *which now appears inevitable.*

I am the deſcendant of ancient Iriſh tribes. Not one of the plundering ſettlers who enſlaved my country ap-pears on the liſt of my anceſtors. They were ſtrenuous defenders of their country's independence: and were the
                                                                    laſt

The opening page of Coigly's memoir, published in 1799.

to promote this alliance. His charismatic personality made him an effective missionary; he was no stranger to the English radicals, nor was this his first attempt to elicit French assistance. He had been to Paris in 1796 and on that occasion had carried with him an address from the 'Secret Committee of England' to the French Directory. In addition, Coigly had a radical social philosophy which was closer to the egalitarianism of the Defenders than to the bourgeois radicalism of the United Irishmen. This alone made him a powerful emissary amongst the disaffected textile workers of Lancashire.

In exile, Coigly served a vital if precarious role, not merely evangelising the British radicals, but acting as a link between the radical United Irish factions in Dublin and Paris. In Manchester he made contact with James Dixon, a cotton spinner from Belfast, who had been instrumental in converting the Manchester Corresponding Society into the oath-bound, republican, United Englishmen. It was here too, that he first met Robert Gray, who became an informer in March 1798. At this meeting, Coigly described himself as an emissary of the United Irish executive, on a second diplomatic mission to Paris where he hoped to secure French assistance for a revolt of 30,000 men. Beyond the city, Coigly assisted the spread of the united system to Stockport, Bolton, Warrington and Birmingham, while further north, contact had been made with the United Scotsmen.

From Manchester, Coigly travelled on to London where he joined the leading activists in the radical conspiracy: Colonel Edward Despard, a native of Queen's County later executed for high treason in 1803; the future Lord Cloncurry, Valentine Lawless, who acted as United Irish representative in the city: and John and Benjamin Binns, key figures in the republican transformation of the Corresponding Society. Coigly attended their meetings at Furnival's Inn, Holborn, where delegates from London, Scotland and the regions outlined their plans, and was entrusted with an address, 'from the chief revolutionary committee of England', outlining their support for a French invasion. This communication, which was subsequently presented to Talleyrand, represented a significant coup for Coigly. Not alone did it reflect the co-operation amongst the British radicals, but it gave an exaggerated appearance of strength and preparation which the priest could exploit in his attempt to secure French military assistance.

Armed with the address, Coigly and Arthur MacMahon, the Presbyterian minister from Holywood, left London for Paris. This journey is outlined in detail in Coigly's *Life*, but any suggestion of its seditious purpose is assiduously avoided. He does, however acknowledge, that an attempted arrest had forced him to dress á la *militaire*. In a similar way, he make little of his meeting with Admiral de Winter on board the fleet at the Texel in the pro-French Batavian

John Binns, a key figure in the republican transformation of the London Corresponding Society.

Republic (Holland); perhaps this absence of comment may have been intended to imply an innocence of the intended destination of this invasion force.

In Paris, as in Ireland, the United Irish ranks were divided. Wolfe Tone and Edward Lewins led the moderate faction, while the radicals took their lead from the veteran campaigner, James Napper Tandy. Lewins was recognised as the official United Irish delegate in the city, but his authority had been challenged since Tandy's arrival from America in June 1797. He had criticised the apparent inactivity of Lewins and Tone, and their position was further weakened by the sudden death, in September, of General Lazare Hoche. Encouraged by the arrival of Coigly, Tandy summoned the two before a mock tribunal; Lewins refused to attend, but Tone who did dismissed it as a 'petty little intrigue'. Having failed to displace the moderates, Coigly was dispatched to Dublin in order to secure Lewins's replacement by a more earnest representative. This would be his final assignment.

Coigly crossed to London via Hamburg where he stayed some days with Samuel Turner of Newry, the United Irish representative in the city. Unknown to the priest, Turner had become an informer and Whitehall was well acquainted with the details of his mission in Britain. Coigly's every movement was monitored by Bow Street runners, and far from being the cunning master of disguise later described by James Anthony Froude, the priest was conspicuous in his military uniform, complete with red cape.

Coigly stayed with the Binns brothers in London and was a frequent visitor at the home of Valentine Lawless. During this short stay, he attended a meeting of the newly formed national committee of the United Britons, on 5 January 1798, and took a fraternal address to the United Irishmen. Together with Benjamin Binns and another member of the committee, William Bailey, he crossed to Ireland. The address was presented to Henry Jackson and it was subsequently discussed at length by a United Irish national committee and circulated to the provinces. The high level of publicity given to it by the radicals reflected their dual intention of spurring the moderates to action and of distracting Whitehall from their Irish activities. Meanwhile, Coigly met with Lord Edward Fitzgerald. The outcome of this meeting appears to have been a commission to replace Lewins at Paris by Arthur O'Connor.

Coigly returned to London in the first week of February. He met with the north of England radicals en route, informing them that this would be his last visit; if he returned it would be to see the tree of liberty planted in Manchester. In London he met with O'Connor at the home of Valentine Lawless where they planned their mission to France. While all three subsequently claimed that this had been their first meeting, they were already well acquainted. Coigly is likely to have collaborated with O'Connor in the Antrim campaign of the previous year and Lawless could hardly have avoided meeting him in London radical circles.

Final preparations were made for this critical mission to France. Three weeks were spent supervising the publication of propaganda and attending radical meetings. On one occasion, Dr Thomas Crossfield, of the London Corresponding Society, entrusted Coigly with an address from 'The secret committee of England' to the Directory of France. This was a high-sounding missive, which according to Froude would appear to any 'solid Englishmen' as the production of a lunatic Yet, in Coigly's hand this address, with its lofty claims could have been the ace. The United Irish interest in British radicalism had been motivated principally by their desire to attract French military assistance to Ireland and, towards this end, the promised welcome for the 'hero of Italy' [Bonaparte] could have been most effective.

The mission to France proved disastrous. Since his arrival at Christmas, O'Connor's high profile amongst the city's Whigs had roused the suspicion of the authorities, who delighted in the prospect of implicating so prominent a friend of the opposition. Even in this attempted flight, O'Connor's arrogance attracted suspicion; not content to allow Coigly to pass as 'Captain Jones', he took the superior title of 'Colonel Morris'. Coupled with this, there was the ludicrous spectacle of this would-be emissary, complete with mountains of luggage, mahogany trunks, hams and other provisions attempting to secure a ferry to France at the height of an invasion scare. Not surprisingly, the party of five—Coigly, John Binns, O'Connor, his servant O'Leary and John Allen, a Dublin United Irishman—were apprehended at the King's Head, Margate, early on 28 February 1798. With characteristic *sang froid*, Coigly asked to finish his breakfast, a request granted by the arresting officers, Fugion and Rivitt, who had trailed him since his return to London in January.

The arrests generated great excitement. In government circles there was delight at the prospect of discrediting the opposition, but the radicals were justifiably anxious. In Paris, Tone expressed amazement; he had little sympathy for Coigly, but dreaded to think of a man of O'Connor's' talents, being caught in such extraordinary circumstances. In Dublin, however, McNally reported that the moderates were not sorry to have the 'impetuous' O'Connor out of the way. The newspapers were filled with accounts of their arrest and the five were reported to be in possession 'a traiterous correspondence' between Ireland, France and England. Fortunately for them, O'Leary with great foresight disposed of the most significant documents in the privy of the *a tavern*. Since these included O'Connor's Paris commission, it was little wonder that Fitzgerald expressed delight that he had 'nothing *odd* with him but twelve hundred guineas'.

The prisoners were brought before the Privy Council, which included both Pitt and the Duke of Portland: O'Connor's mahogany trunk was opened, revealing little of importance, save for a code which made sense only after Lord Edward's later arrest. In spite of this disappointment, the government resolved to act. On 12 March, almost the entire Leinster provincial committee was arrested in a raid on Oliver Bond's house, along with members of its executive, in what Tone called 'the most terrible blow...a triumph for Fitzgibbon'. This was followed by the capture of the leading English radicals in swoops in Manchester, Leicester and Birmingham on 18 and 19 April.

The difficulty for government was that most of the evidence against the Margate five consisted of informers' reports which would be inadmissible in court without revealing the identity of Turner, McNally and other valuable sources. Accordingly, the trial was delayed until mid-May: in the interim a frantic search for 'such evidence of guilt as will suffice to convict them in the ordinary course of law' was mounted. Government intelligence increased; the confessions of Robert Gray confirmed the prisoners' guilt; there were rumours that O'Connor offered to turn King's evidence; attempts were made to use Coigly's confessor to secure additional information; Coigley himself was offered his life if only he would implicate O'Connor.

Such was the urgency of the Dublin administration that the trial began on 20 May before sufficient evidence had been assembled. The entire case rested on Dr Crossfield's address which had been found in the pocket of Coigly's coat. From the outset the prejudice of the court was evident. It soon emerged that Revd. Arthur Young, son of the famed traveller, had attempted to sway prospective jurors, stressing the necessity 'for the security of the realm' that 'the felons should swing' irrespective of their innocence or guilt. O'Connor, who had attempted to bribe the jailers, mounted a spirited defence, to the point where he was reprimanded by Justice Buller for prejudicing the case of the other defendants. In any event, his ability to call Charles James Fox and the Whig establishment in his defence was sufficient to dazzle the jury and assure his acquittal.

Against Coigly, the Crown called Frederick Dutton, a notorious criminal and perjurer from Newry who may have been recommended by Samuel Turner. His principal task was to identify the priest's hand writing and he duly obliged, claiming to have seen it on a lottery ticket at Dundalk. Having performed this task, he was awarded £50 expenses, the equivalent of almost two years wages. Coigly was hardly allowed a defence and what representation he had was made possible only by the generosity of Valentine Lawless. Two defence witnesses, Bernard Coyle and Valentine Derry were requested, but neither of these were called. The odds were stacked against the priest; his companions were acquitted, but he was found guilty on the most slender evidence, the presence of the letter in his coatpocket. Sentencing him to death, Justice Buller praised the mildness and clemency of the administration. At that point Coigly took a pinch of snuff and said 'ahem!'

The conviction was a pyrrhic victory for the administration. O'Connor, the important prisoner, had been acquitted, the government had failed in its effort to implicate the opposition and the unsatisfactory nature of the trial had made a martyr of the Armagh priest. Nowhere was the anger more keenly felt than in Dublin Castle and John Fitzgibbon cursed Young's 'foolish rhapsody' which Edward Cooke believed had saved the lives of the prisoners who were acquitted. The satisfaction of Whig opposition, however, was short-lived, since O'Connor's admission of guilt before the Irish parliamentry Committees of Secrecy the following August exposed the folly of their court appearances.

In the interim, the opposition press exploited the spectacle of Coigly's execution. In a skilfully directed campaign every effort was made to present the dignity and integrity of an innocent victim. In this choreographed drama Coigly played his part to perfection; even on the scaffold he denounced the 'church and king mob' of his native county. Tone, receiving the news of Coigly's execution exclaimed, 'nothing in his life became him like the leaving of it'.

In Ireland Coigly's death was overtaken by events. Rebellion had broken out on 23 May and in those critical circumstances news of the priest's death made little impact.

Chapter Five

'Close enough to toss a ship's biscuit ashore': The French fleet at Bantry Bay, 1796

Stephen McGarry

In 1796 a large French invasion fleet slipped past the royal navy and moored off the south-west coast of Ireland at Bantry Bay. Battered by storms, the French troops were unable to land and returned to France. 'We were close enough to toss a ship's biscuit ashore', wrote Theobald Wolfe Tone bitterly in his diary.

France and Britain had been at war since 1793 and the French Republic contemplated an invasion of Ireland, believing that Britain's naval superiority would be reduced by the loss of Ireland. The Society of United Irishmen, which aimed to bring about an independent Irish republic, was driven underground in 1794. The following year Theobald Wolfe Tone fled to France and lobbied for French support for an invasion of Ireland. He argued that Ireland was the least defensible part of the British Isles and he was fortunate to find a willing ally in the acclaimed Anglophobic general Lazare Hoche. The French recovered faded naval charts written in parchment from their archives, some dating back to the mid-seventeenth century, and dusted them off as they gamely considered the proposal. 'To detach Ireland from England is to reduce England to a second-rate power, and take from it much of its maritime superiority', concluded one of the French war ministers as he gave the go-ahead. 'There is little point in elaborating on the advantage to France that Irish independence would bring'.

L'Expédition d'Irlande, due to depart in September 1796, was dogged by delays. But by December a 43-ship fleet, comprising seventeen ships of the line, thirteen frigates, corvettes and transport ships, commanded by Vice-Admiral Justin-Bonaventure Morand de Galles, together with 13,975 veteran troops under General Lazare Hoche, stood ready at the Atlantic seaport of Brest in Brittany. The remaining regiments of the old Irish Brigade of France were disbanded after the French Revolution in 1789, lost their distinctive red uniforms and were absorbed into the regular French army, although for many years after they were still regarded as 'Irish regiments'. Although none of them accompanied the Bantry Bay expedition, a number of high-ranking former Irish Brigade officers did. Major-General Oliver Harty from Limerick commanded a unit. Other senior Irish officers present were *Général de Brigade* Richard O'Shea from Cork and Lt Col Andrew McDonagh from Sligo. A newly activated Irish corps called the *Légion Irlandaise* (not to be confused with Napoleon's Irish unit created several years later) did sail that winter, officered by Irishmen or men of Irish descent, dressed in red with facings in green, evoking the famous red-coated Irish Brigade of old, but didn't register more than one battalion.

On the mild morning of 16 December, the signal was given to 'heave short', as the ships' cables were pulled short over their anchors; two hours later anchors were weighed and the fleet cleared port. A number of ships collided with each other as they sailed out, indicative of poor seamanship, which many saw as a bad omen. Vice-Admiral Morand de Galles, aware of the Royal Navy lurking off the Breton coast, intended to sail south at night through a dangerous narrow channel, the Raz de Seine. This was a decoy manoeuvre to fool the Royal Navy into believing that his destination was Portugal. The Raz, however, proved to be too dangerous to navigate in the darkness; the *Séduisant* (74 guns) ran aground off the rocks. Morand de Galles instead ordered the ships in the rear to head westerly towards the Iroise Channel, thus splitting the fleet. The French fleet had slipped past the principal Royal Navy squadron blockading Brest, but their departure had not been unobserved. Earlier in December, Captain Sir Edward Pellow's frigate squadron and local spies had seen increased activity at Brest and anchored at Falmouth to notify the Admiralty that the French were about to take to the sea. Two of Pellow's frigates later encountered the man-o'-war *Droite de l'Homme* (74 guns) and raked her with fire; she struck her colours before the storm broke her stern, with the loss of over 1,000 lives. Lord Bridport's Channel Fleet, anchored at Spithead outside Portsmouth, was scrambled but returned to port owing to a strong westerly wind.

On the morning of 19 December, seventeen ships, including Tone's, the man-o'-war *Indomptable* (80 guns), waited as the remaining fleet emerged through the heavy fog. A number of ships were missing; crucially, there was no sign of the flagship *Fraternité* (32 guns), carrying the two commanders-in-chief, Morand de Galles and Hoche. She had been blown off course by strong winds, only to return to France. The fleet separated again but joined up and continued cruising along the Irish coast. When nine nautical miles off Cape Clear, Tone caught sight of his native land and saw patches of snow on the mountains, and later on a number of castles scattered in the countryside.

They arrived at the rendezvous point off Mizen Head on 21 December and opened their sealed orders, written by Morand and Hoche, containing the location of the proposed landing—Bantry Bay. They were to disembark there and march on Cork, join forces with the United Irishmen and their supporters and push northwards. (This was the second major force dispatched to Bantry since the Spanish Armada. During the Jacobite War, in 1689, the French navy engaged an English fleet and landed there with supplies of arms.)

The fleet coasted close to Mizen before standing out to sea for their approach to Bantry Bay. French fortunes changed when off Dursey Island they picked up a number of Irish pilots, who had sailed out in a hooker in the belief that the French ships were British. Nevertheless, they agreed to guide them into the bay. The French ships, pitching and rolling, tacked for hours in the strong easterly head winds but made little progress as they navigated Bantry's natural harbour, with only fifteen ships, including Tone's and the *Immortalité* (40 guns), carrying General Emmanuel de Grouchy, the second-in-command, entering the bay. The frigate *Résolue* (32 guns) collided with another ship and launched a longboat to tow her, but it was blown ashore and taken as a prize, along with one Lt Prointeau and his crew. Meanwhile, the ships outside the bay's mouth dropped anchor when the gale developed into a storm that lasted two days, preventing their passage into the bay; others were blown back into the open sea.

General de Grouchy convened a council of war, intending to capture Cork with the remaining 6,500 troops and to follow Tone's plan for an amphibious landing in Sligo Bay with a regiment of the *Legion des Francs*, a company of light artillery and as many officers, stores and arms as they could spare. An order of battle was briskly drawn up. 'We have nothing but the arms in our hands', Tone wrote with gusto in his diary, 'the clothes on our back, and a good courage, but that is sufficient'.

Admiral Sir Robert Kingsmill's frigate squadron, based in their home port of Cork, was not strong enough to confront the French. On Christmas Eve, Kingsmill ordered Flag Lt Pulling to the Bantry area to see what was happening. Pulling boarded a cutter and peered at the fleet through his telescope; in the closing darkness and dense haze he couldn't see any flags or pennants but concluded that 'I am certain [they] were not English ships'. The Cork squadron went on to take the *Ville de L'Orient*, armed *en flute*, with 400 hussars on board, which was later towed into Kinsale as a prize amid great excitement.

A heavy gale, however, blew on Christmas Eve night. Tone's ship remained rolling heavily in the bay, the wind roaring through the rigging as the ship creaked and groaned, the waves crashing violently against her hull. Tone, unable to sleep, got out of his hanging 'cot', put on his boots and greatcoat, and paced the *Indomptable*'s quarterdeck. He worried that the strong easterly gales blowing from the shore, accompanied by snow, would not only make it impossible to land but also prevent them from posting a frigate at the harbour's mouth to warn of the arrival of any English ships. Tone was a lawyer and knew that he was committing high treason; if captured, he surmised, he would be subject to a public trial and then hung, drawn and quartered as a warning to others—unless, of course, he had the good fortune to be killed in action.

In the evening of Christmas Day, de Grouchy's frigate suddenly emerged out of the stormy darkness and scudded at speed under the quarterdeck of Tone's ship, an officer shouting through a semaphore 'with orders to cut our cable and put to sea instantly'. Was this a *ruse de guerre*, Tone wrote in disbelief? Perhaps it was an English frigate masquerading as a French ship? But de Grouchy's ship left the bay, 'and the fog is so thick', wrote Tone in disgust, 'that we cannot see a ship's length, we are left without admiral or general'.

Strong easterly and south-easterly gale-force winds continued to blow the next day, battering the fleet. The *Indomptable* dropped her fore and aft anchors to keep her position but they still dragged on the sea floor, nearly blowing the ship onto the rocks. The *Révolution* (74 guns) rocked and swayed violently under the strain as another heavy sea swell lifted it, could hold no longer, cut her cable and put to sea, followed swiftly by several others. There were now only seven men-o'-war and one frigate in the bay. As the winds were now against the fleet moving up towards Sligo, Major-General Oliver Harty, as the most senior officer present, convened a council of war; they agreed to sail further up the coast with just over 4,000 men, two four-pounders and ammunition, and wait for the rest of the fleet.

The ships cruised along the coast and moored at the mouth of the Shannon, until a 'dreadful hurricane' blew up on 28 December, battering and nearly sinking Tone's ship. The huge waves crested and crashed over the decks, plunging the cabins into darkness and filling them with water up to their waists. The following day, the signal was given for the nine remaining ships to steer for France. The frigate *Scévola* (44 guns) foundered, but luckily all 820 men on board were rescued by the *Révolution*; the demasted frigate *Impatiente* (40 guns) was wrecked off Crookhaven with all hands, save for seven, while *Surveilance* was leaking water and was scuttled. Tone, desperately disappointed, spent the day seasick in his cabin, his ship arriving back in Brest on 1 January, 'astonished that we hadn't seen an English ship, going or coming back'. The British army in Ireland was caught off guard. 'We had, two days after they were at anchor in Bantry Bay, from Cork to Bantry less than 3,000 men, two pieces of artillery, and no magazine of any kind, no firings, no hospital, no provisions, etc,' reported one contemporary English account. The commander of the British army in Cork, Lt Gen William Dalrymple, now headquartered at nearby Bantry House, wrote that they were hopelessly unprepared, and even with 8,000 troops in Cork would not have confronted the French: 'Our numbers will probably fall so short of the enemy, that a diversion is all to be expected'.

Only 35 ships returned to Brest, many badly damaged, with over 1,500 drowned and 2,000 captured. De Grouchy should not have split the fleet by changing his orders as the fleet travelled through the Raz. Hoche should have boarded a three-master, not a smaller frigate, and if he had remained with the fleet he would have acted more decisively than his second-in-command, Morand de Galles. Of course, the strong easterly gales off the tempestuous south-west Irish coast didn't help; neither did poor French seamanship. In 1798 the French tried again and landed an expeditionary force on the west coast of Ireland, which also ended in failure. Tone was aboard a French ship intercepted by the Royal Navy off the Donegal coast and captured. He fought gallantly, commanding a gun battery in the action, but alas had not 'the good fortune to be killed in the action', as he wrote two years previously in his diary. He was brought to Dublin, found guilty of treason and sentenced to be hanged, cheating the hangman's noose by cutting his own throat.

Chapter Six

A 'Catholic wind' on Bantry Bay?

Gordon Kennedy

On Christmas Day 1796, while Theobald Wolfe Tone was still anxiously pacing the deck of a French warship, desperately hoping that Lazare Hoche's subordinates would actually come to a decision and land the depleted force of revolutionary troops that were seeking shelter below decks, the Catholic bishop of Cork, Francis Moylan, delivered a pastoral to his flock. While previous pastorals of the Catholic hierarchy had contained similar pleas to remain loyal and steadfast to king and country, Moylan's was more vociferous in tone and apparently effective. Furthermore, it could have earned him a severe, and possibly fatal, penalty had the expeditionary force landed in any great numbers.

Moylan's pastoral was widely welcomed in loyalist circles. Robert Day, MP for Tuam, described it as 'breathing a spirit of peace and loyalty worthy of an apostle'. To him, Moylan had not 'balanced between duty and danger' in his swift call to resist the French 'invader'. To packed Christmas congregations, Moylan urged his Catholic brethren to rally to the king's standard and to reject the 'irreparable ruin, desolation and destruction occasioned by French fraternity'. In a grim warning to the people filling the pews, he stated that any 'contrary conduct will draw inevitable ruin on you here and eternal misery hereafter'. He stated his belief that Catholic emancipation was imminent and that the worst of their distresses were already consigned to history; 'for blessed be God, we are no longer strangers in our own native land, no longer excluded from the benefits of the happy constitution under which we live, no longer separated by odious distinctions from our fellow subjects'. Regardless of certain expedient inaccuracies, the pastoral seems to have had the desired effect. No signal fires welcomed Hoche's experienced veterans; there was no rapturous welcome as promised by Tone.

Tone's diary tells us that vicious storms and French indecisiveness were the direct causes of the expedition's failure. To underestimate the power of hierarchical censure in the immediate context of that December would, however, be unwise and counter-intuitive. As Jeremiah Collins revealed in his

General Lazare Hoche's December 1796 proclamation to his troops, stressing the need for discipline during the Irish campaign.

funeral oration for Moylan in 1815, the pastoral of 1796 contained a power that 'inspired the multitude with an order and a prowess to defend their country, their altars and their homes'. Bishop Moylan, in return for his loyal pastoral, received the freedom of Cork city and unanimous praise from politicians and clergy alike. Monsignor Erskine, the papal representative in London, wrote to Moylan, congratulating him on the gallantry he had shown during the attempt by the 'common enemy to invade'. He also informed him that he was sending a copy of the pastoral to the pope as proof that the 'spiritual direction of the

Le Degraisseur Patriote

Patience Monsieur votre tour viendra   *Le Preſſoir*   *Il n'i a plus de remede*

A contemporary French cartoon depicting Le Degraisseur Patriote ('the patriotic de-fattening machine'). Revolutionary images such as this terrified Moylan and the Irish hierarchy.

Catholics of Ireland is committed to such hands as can, and will, preserve them from all contagion'.

The pastoral was not merely a spontaneous warning by Moylan against a lately manifested threat or the means to ingratiate himself into favour. Moylan could speak with some authority on the French revolutionary order, given the fact that he had been educated there and had received explicit (albeit highly partisan) accounts of its excesses from his close friend Abbé Edgeworth, King Louis XVI's confessor. Moylan passionately believed that religion itself was under threat from revolutionary change and that the people of Ireland were being duped by radical incendiaries into political beliefs that they could neither comprehend nor understand. It was a classic example of the paternalistic instinct with which the Catholic clergy of that time were imbued; the 'natural' leaders of the Catholic multitudes needed to scold the wavering and damn the disaffected.

Lord Camden was so impressed with Moylan's words of loyalty that he suggested that the pastoral should be translated into Irish and circulated around the kingdom in an attempt to defuse potential sedition in the aftermath of the French attempt on Ireland. Privately, the United Irishmen simply dismissed Moylan's stance as 'pious fraud', the rantings of a craven snake-oil salesman. Publicly, however, they had to be mindful of venting their disgust at 'Castle

Catholics', lest they alienate recruitment into their ranks by espousing Jacobin-style anti-clericalism. Besides, they took heart that the French, having shown serious commitment towards the liberation of Ireland, would return to arm and assist their planned revolution.

There were some dissenting voices, however, within the Catholic hierarchy concerning the deferential tone of Moylan's words. In 1797, Bishop Thomas Hussey from the neighbouring Waterford diocese drew much criticism from his contemporaries when he publicly condemned the proselytising practices of militia officers on their mostly Catholic recruits. A critical letter from Moylan to Hussey brought about a withering response from the Waterford prelate. Hussey reminded Moylan that his 1796 pastoral had produced few concessions from the government on the Catholic question except 'a declaration that Catholics should wear the remaining chains to the end of the world'. It is not recorded how Moylan reacted to this remark but it can be imagined that it irked the Corkman considerably, given the fact that there were already rumours on the ground that he was in receipt of a Castle pension for his stance in 1796.

While Hussey's complaints garnered support from the laity, the Catholic hierarchy worried that any perceived criticism of Crown forces' behaviour could undermine and eventually scupper their ongoing appeals for full emancipation. The old formula remained the best avenue for change—loyalty to king and country—and this sat very comfortably on the shoulders of the bishop of Cork. To radicals and revolutionaries, this provided further proof that the hierarchy had indeed been bought off by the Castle with the establishment of the Cathjolic seminary at Maynooth in 1795. In their eyes, its annual subsidy from government merely confirmed that the clergy were blatantly compromised and thus tightly controlled by the Castle 'junto'. In Moylan's eyes, the establishment of the seminary was crucial to the infrastructure of Catholicism in a country emerging from penal persecution. To him, it was a blessing that should 'excite our gratitude and unshaken loyalty to our gracious sovereign, a sovereign who [had] done more for the Catholic body and this kingdom than any or all of his predecessors'. However obsequious these sentiments may appear today, they were forcefully held by the hierarchical establishment during this period of white-hot smothered rebellion. Loyalty was also a sound tactic of self-preservation. It was far better to trust in gradual Catholic emancipation than in a new revolutionary order established by 'atheistical incendiaries'.

Less is known about the effect of the 1796 pastoral on the ordinary Catholics of County Cork, but it is notable that it was one of the areas least affected by the rebellion that erupted seventeen months later. The Burkean philosophy that if you had the loyalty of the bishops then you had the loyalty of the people seemed to have paid dividends for the establishment. This was particularly evident in Munster during 1798. Apart from the obvious martial reasons for this apparent apathy, the Castle was very aware that the hierarchy had come good for them in the final showdown. Moylan benefited personally from his loyal exertions during these critical years. He replaced Thomas Hussey as the main intermediary between the Catholic hierarchy and eminent politicians such as Castlereagh, Portland and Pitt. The goodwill and heartfelt loyalty displayed by Moylan during the United Irish crisis was harnessed by Pitt and Cornwallis. They needed him and the rest of the hierarchy to push for Catholic acceptance of a union that was linked to full Catholic emancipation.

On this political issue, however, Francis Moylan was a disappointed man when he died on 10 February 1815. After all the professions of loyalty during the 1790s, the support of various Castle administrations and for the Union itself, the holy grail of emancipation looked as far off as ever as he lay on his deathbed. Moylan the pastor had succeeded spectacularly in the re-emergence of a Catholic infrastructure in Munster, but Moylan the politician had failed in the ultimate goal of guiding his people to full emancipation by peaceful means. That measure did not arrive until 1829, fourteen years after his death. Nevertheless, a sturdy foundation had been laid to build the type of Catholic clerical ascendancy that was so evident in the late nineteenth and early twentieth centuries.

Chapter Seven

A rough guide to revolutionary Paris: Wolfe Tone as an accidental tourist

Sylvie Kleinman

On a cold day in March 1796 Aristide Du Petit Thouars, a *ci-devant* French aristocrat and naval officer just returned from exile in America, visited the Panthéon in the heart of Paris. In his absence France had undergone the Revolution, but with the Terror over, the Bastille torn down and the five-man Directory in power, his homeland had become a somewhat 'less obnoxious country', to borrow an earlier comment of Pitt's. A very harsh winter and inevitable food shortages were compounded by galloping inflation and the ongoing war with Britain. Yet despite public apathy, Paris had replaced Versailles as the magnet of cultural and social life under a regime synonymous with eccentric fashions and the pursuit of pleasure. Most importantly, the mid-1790s were the backdrop to Napoleon's meteoric rise to power.

The Frenchman was showing the sights of a capital transformed by the turbulent events of recent years to James Smith, an American merchant whom he had befriended during the stormy transatlantic crossing from America. To ward off their fleecing innkeeper in the seaport of Le Havre, he later wrote to his sister, 'mon bon Américain Smith' had insisted on lending him one *louis*, and so to settle this debt they had met up again in Paris. Smith privately despised aristocrats and unearned privilege, but couldn't help liking this Frenchman who had known many adventures and reversals of fortune. The Panthéon itself, formerly the Church of Ste-Geneviève, embodied the dynamic clash between their two worlds. In 1791 it had been transformed into a republican, secular resting-place for the ashes of the great men of the era of French liberty. After viewing the cenotaphs of Voltaire and Rousseau, they climbed to the viewing terrace and enjoyed a spectacular panorama of Paris, which was covered in a foot of snow.

Their paths would cross again in January 1797, in what seemed to the Frenchman the most unlikely place, the naval port of Brest. Du Petit Thouars, now a commodore, was astounded to bump into Smith now sporting the

La Grande Galerie du Louvre in 1796 (though when Tone visited the skylights had not yet been added) – Tone enjoyed visiting the newly created Muséum Central des Arts housed here, where admission was free. (RMN, Paris)

uniform of a French *chef de brigade*. He had just returned from the ill-fated Bantry Bay expedition because, he boldly stated, he was really an Irishman, and his mission was to free his country from the yoke of tyranny. His actions were treasonable, and if he were caught he would be hanged. The Frenchman was deeply moved by the episode.

Smith was the pseudonym used by Theobald Wolfe Tone, whose mission to France remains one of the most daring in Irish history. Torn from loved ones, forced to lie low and to maintain a false identity, frustrated with endless hours to fill, and defensively reacting to the necessary linguistic and cultural assimilation into his country of asylum, he turned to his diary. It meanders between optimism and despair, the trivial and the grave, but is also peppered with astute observations on people he met and places he saw. This witty and moving chronicle of Tone's experiences, along with his autobiography, has been widely read since its publication in 1826. But the political impact of his writings and the iconic status to which he was posthumously elevated as the 'father of Irish republicanism' have overshadowed a rich and vibrant dimension to this written legacy. The eighteenth century had witnessed an unprecedented increase in human mobility and curiosity about other places, and Tone had been born into the golden age of travel writing. His mission to France, sojourn in Paris and military service in French-occupied Germany, Flanders and Holland from 1796 to 1798 unfolded against the backdrop of the war with Britain. Thus he was privileged to travel through parts of the Continent closed to the leisurely voyager, and, like many a diplomat and soldier, become an accidental tourist and a diarist-chronicler of history.

Like many tourists, essentials like food and lodgings were prioritised, and Tone energetically countered rumours in the English press that France was starving her people. Before leaving Philadelphia he had exchanged £100 into *louis d'or* or gold coin, and this gave him greater purchasing power than the revolutionary but now inflated paper money, or *assignats*, and the opportunity to bail out a former aristocrat. Generally he found food cheap and plentiful, and his 'superb crimson damask bed' at the main hotel in Le Havre only amounted to the equivalent of tenpence a day. French complaints about the coarse brown bread (*pain bis*) were irritating, and so he enthusiastically devised a toast to his mission: *Vive le pain bis et la liberté!*

For many travellers, getting one's message across in a foreign language is one of the most problematic aspects of experiencing cultural difference. Betsy Sheridan had once noted that a brogue does not transfer into French, allowing the Irish to 'blend in', and so for Tone it was essential to speak the language to remain *incognito* (as he repeatedly noted). He must indeed have had a perceptible accent, as later in Paris the American ambassador's secretary immediately detected that he was Irish when handing him back his (false) American passport. Thus a vital dimension to Tone's legend begins within hours of his setting foot in France, namely that he claimed that he could not speak French. When he met Napoleon Bonaparte in December 1797, the Corsican had asked him about his competence in the language, and Tone had replied (and more or less lied) that he had only learned the little French he knew since his arrival in France. He resented being reliant on others to communicate, and melodramatically cast himself as the victim of a typical eighteenth-century narrative of misfortune. Was he not to be pitied, alone and unable to speak the language? It didn't take long for him to be ripped off for his first bad meal, and he was furious that he couldn't scold in French.

Tone's narrative of his journey from Le Havre to Paris reads more like classic travel literature. Thanks to the pace of the horse-drawn carriage, travellers could comment on the countryside, and so Tone admired upper Normandy and 'the Seine winding beautifully thro' the landscape'. He found the land well

The Fête des Victoires on the Champ de Mars, in honour of the recent French victories in Italy, 29 May 1796 – according to Tone, 'A superb spectacle … I was placed at the foot of the Altar in the middle of my brethren of the Corps Diplomatique [though he] chose to remain incognito'.

cultivated (but in 1797 would be far more impressed with Dutch agricultural practice), and passed several chateaux shut up or deserted. In a delicious irony, he mocked himself travelling in 'a choice carriage lined with blue velvet', like an English lord. He was, after all, the elder son of a Dublin coachmaker.

Shortly after his arrival in Paris, Tone mocked himself as the Irish 'minister plenipotentiary planning a revolution', yet he undertook his mission with seriousness of purpose and dogged determination. The French authorities had been made aware of his imminent arrival, true identity and purpose in praiseworthy dispatches from their envoy in Philadelphia, and he was granted permission to stay. His official contacts were at the highest level but, in sharp contrast, the rest of his time was spent alone, as he had been advised to keep a very low profile. For a naturally gregarious man who thrived on convivial conversation the enforced isolation was at times intolerable. Born and raised in Dublin, he had spent two years in his early twenties (reluctantly) studying law in London, and so had already experienced urban life in an 'idle and luxurious capital', and despite bouts of loneliness and despair he appeared comfortable in Paris: 'Walked about Paris diverting myself innocently… I wish I could once more see the green sod of Ireland! Yet Paris is delightful!' (21 April 1796).

Tone arrived at the Messageries Nationales in the 2nd arrondissement and there his papers would have been checked. Foreigners had to carry their passports wherever they went, but it also meant that they could gain free admission to some of the sights in Paris. Before finding private lodgings, he stayed in the nearby Hôtel des Étrangers on the Rue Vivienne, one of the finest and most expensive in Paris. That part of the Right Bank was becoming increasingly fashionable, and he was only 'within fifty yards' of the notorious Palais-Royal gardens, now renamed the Maison-Égalité. Tone would have strolled under its arcades, lined with many shops, cafés and the increasingly popular restaurants, but would also have passed gambling dens and bawdy houses. He was aware that this former rendezvous of the *beau monde* had degenerated, discreetly switching into French in his diary to record that it was swarming with innumerable women of pleasure. Also plying their trade on the Rue Vivienne were money speculators, whom Tone appropriately described as *agioteurs*, the term specifically 'coined' for them. The numerous booksellers became a favourite haunt, however, and there he picked up a copy of the new French constitution, as well as many military books, 'dog cheap'. The Revolution had democratised eating out as we now know it (though mainly for the rising bourgeoisie), and Tone was lucky to be within walking distance of the finest *restaurateurs* of the capital. So impressed was he with his first meal in Paris (but adding that he was ashamed to say so much about eating) that he appended a translated bill of fare, which totalled '£0.4.7½ ster[lin]g'. Two nights later he dined in the superb Méot's, 'in a room covered with gilding and looking glasses down to the floor'. It was the former home of the chancellor to the duc d'Orléans and much misery of the people had gone into ornamenting it, he commented, yet now anyone could dine there for the equivalent of 3s. Even in his wildest dreams he could not have imagined that he would be back at Méot's in November 1797 with other United Irishmen hosting a celebratory dinner for General Desaix after his victory at Kehl.

Many of his idle wanderings doubled as tourism, and with Du Petit Thouars he had spent an entire day exploring the revolutionised capital. Many place-names had been changed to reflect the new order: the Place Vendôme was renamed the Place des Piques, and what is today the Place des Vosges was the Place des Fédérés and an artillery store filled with cannon. They enjoyed the 'vast collection of curious exotics' at the new Museum of Natural History, and crossed the Seine to see the place where the Bastille once stood (now a timber yard) and the Temple where Louis XVI and Marie-Antoinette had been imprisoned. Its gloomy appearance made Tone melancholy. Every day he strolled down to the now public and fashionable Tuileries gardens, also the site of much turbulence but now *the* place to be seen, as the Directory had commissioned restoration and landscaping works. There Tone praised the appearance of French women but couldn't make sense of the current fashion for wigs, which he found ludicrous. Not once did he comment on the diaphanous

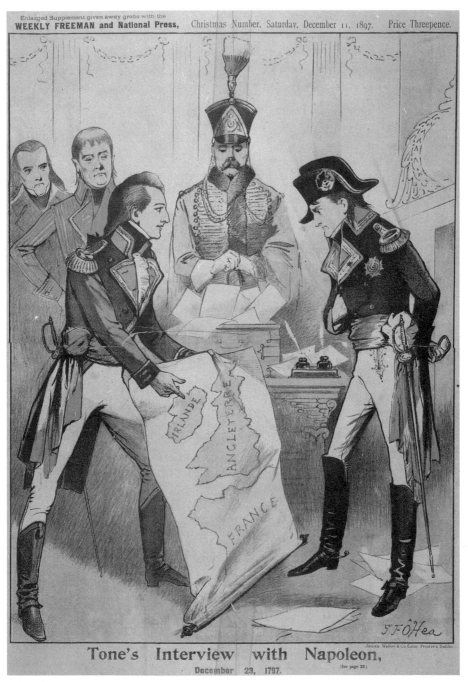

Tone's interview with Napoleon, 23 December 1797 – the Corsican asked Tone about his competence in French, and he replied that he had only learned the little he knew since his arrival in France. (Weekly Freeman & National)

and perilously low-cut Grecian-style dresses for which the Directory period became famous. He preferred looking at soldiers and was especially drawn to the changing of the guards and the appearance of officers, as he had nurtured since boyhood an untameable desire to become a soldier.

Tone enjoyed visiting the newly created Muséum Central des Arts, housed in the Louvre Palace, where admission was free. Opened on 10 August 1793, its galleries quickly filled with works seized from the church or fleeing émigrés, war trophies brought home by the Republic's triumphant armies, and the royal collections transferred from Versailles. It should be noted, however, that Tone's visits in the spring of 1796 pre-dated Napoleon's massive plunder of Italian and Egyptian artworks. Housing the nation's cultural heritage was problematic, and, as the former palace was undergoing major construction works in 1796, the museum was closed on his first visit. He was impressed, however, that he was allowed in after stating that he was a foreigner, as foreigners were encouraged to experience national improvements.

Tone admired paintings by Guido Reni, Rembrandt, Raphael and Van Dyck. It is likely that some of the works he saw were part of the 1794 booty 'appropriated' for the French people by the armies of the North and Sambre et Meuse. Later, as a French officer stationed in Cologne, he made a casual but revealing comment after attending Easter Mass in the cathedral, acknowledging the practice of plunder: 'I fancy they have concealed their plate and ornaments for fear of us, and they are much right in that'. He would not have seen the *Mona Lisa* in the Louvre, as it was only transferred from Versailles in 1797; in any case, it was then still an obscure work and not the merchandising icon of today. Tone did take a day trip out to Versailles, which, *inter alia*, prompted an indignant outburst on the monotony of French gardens.

One painting in particular captivated Tone, and we may find his taste perplexing, and not just for esthetic reasons. It was an opulent full-length portrait of *The Penitent Magdalene* by the great Baroque painter Charles le Brun. Painted *c.* 1650, its almost theatrical intensity would have appealed to late eighteenth-century tastes for sentimental depictions, and it portrays the moment when the sinner renounces her ill-gotten material pleasures. She dramatically looks up to heaven with her forsaken jewels strewn at her feet:

> The *Magdalen* of le Brun is, in my mind, worth the whole collection. I never saw anything in the way of painting which came near it. I am no artist, but it requires no previous instruction to be struck with the numberless beauties of this most enchanting piece. It is a production of consummate genius (6 March 1796).

Tone claims to have returned a second time and to have spent close to an hour staring at it.

The theatre (including opera and ballet) was a nightly refuge for Tone, whether in major cities or provincial towns in every country he visited. Tone contextualised the performing arts under the Directory as a state-subsidised propaganda exercise. In Le Havre he commented on the dénouement of a popular anti-religious play, *Les rigueurs du cloître* (1790). Its plot typically revolves around lovers separated by monastery walls, but the convent is stormed by the valiant National Guards, who not only set the young ladies free but requisition the property for the nation. On his second night in Paris he attended a ballet called *L'offrande à la liberté*, which perfectly illustrates how martial valour had permeated many aspects of French culture. It re-enacted the most important French republican festival, the Feast of the Federation, held on 14 July 1790 at the purpose-built grounds on the Champs de Mars. These bizarre and pompous ceremonies had been devised to instil a cult of faith in the fatherland as a replacement for religion. The ballet featured an altar of Liberty centre-stage, and female characters in beautiful Grecian habits who presented sabres to young men in regimentals. Tone was enthralled by the military evolutions and processions, and mused that, whatever 'Mr Burke may think, the age of chivalry is not gone in France'. Theatre managers were compelled to play patriotic songs, and most shows concluded with the *Marseillaise*. Because Tone records the reaction of the audience, he must have been aware that the police were monitoring the public mood and issuing reports of the *esprit publique* in the press.

But on 29 May he was to witness at first hand a genuine republican ceremony, as he had been invited to attend the Fête des Victoires on the Champs de Mars in honour of the recent French victories in Italy. Only ten days earlier the authorities had granted renewed permission to stay to this *réfugié Irlandais*, and he had received a VIP invitation. At the splendid fête he was 'placed at the foot of the altar in the middle of my brethren of the Corps Diplomatique', though he 'chose to remain *incognito*'. The Directory and ministers all attended in ceremonial costume, and 6,000 troops represented the armies of the Republic. The handsomest grenadier of each corps had a standard and a garland of oak presented to him by Carnot, the Director for War, and Tone was moved to tears at this spectacle 'worthy of a great republic'.

By summer Tone would no longer be a passive spectator at such displays of the citizen-soldier's commitment to the nation, as on 17 July he received his long-awaited commission as a *chef de brigade d'infanterie* (with the rank of colonel). Apart from his strategic role as a sort of project manager for the Irish expeditions, and despite negative self-assessments of his French, Tone had become at this stage a functional bilingual. Like many lesser-known Irish officers throughout the centuries, he demonstrated his practical usefulness by translating documents and acting as a liaison interpreter. Tone's papers, scattered in various French archives, demonstrate such a remarkably high standard of French that it is difficult to accept his own 'evidence' that he had never studied the language before 1796.

Only recently has Du Petit Thouars's personal testimonial of 'James Smith' been discovered, confirming how clandestine Tone's mission truly had been. In his autobiography, Tone boasted that he and his sibling possessed an inexplicable 'romantic spirit of adventure', and his *voyage de guerre* allowed him to live it to the full. When thinking of the fate that awaited him, and his presence on that cold afternoon in the French Panthéon, it must be remembered that it is also the final resting-place of many a great writer. The publication of the final volume of the scholarly edition of Tone's *Writings*, enriched with innumerable annotations and a long-awaited index, allows us to savour fully this unexplored cultural gem embedded in a canon of Irish national literature.

Chapter Eight

A forgotten army: The Irish Yeomanry

Allan Blackstock

In September 1796, Ireland was pregnant with expectation. The United Irishmen and Defenders planned insurrection and a French invasion was imminent. On 19 September Dublin Castle announced plans to follow Britain's lead and enlist civilian volunteers as a yeomanry force. In October commissions were issued to local gentlemen and magistrates empowering them to raise cavalry troops and infantry companies. Recruits took the 'Yeomanry oath' and were officered by the local gentry, but were paid, clothed, armed and controlled by government. Their remit was to free the regular army and militia from domestic peacekeeping and do garrison duty if invasion meant troops had to move to the coast. Service was part-time—usually two 'exercise days' per week—except during emergencies when they were called up on 'permanent duty'.

If the Irish Yeomanry are remembered at all it is usually for their notoriety in the bloody summer of 1798. The popular folk memory of every area which saw action supplies lurid stories from the burning of Father John Murphy's corpse in a tar barrel at Tullow in County Wexford, to the sabreing and mutilation of Betsy Gray after the battle of Ballynahinch in County Antrim. Until recently, the Yeomen have been largely written out of history, apart from early nineteenth century polemics where they appear either as a brutal mob making 'croppies' lie down or latter day Williamite saviours. Such neglect belies the Irish Yeomanry's real significance.

When Belfast's White Linen Hall was demolished in 1896 to make way for City Hall a glass phial containing a scroll bearing Volunteer reform resolutions was found in its foundations. Two years later another demolition occurred. Ballynahinch loyalists smashed the monument on Betsy Gray's grave to prevent a 1798 centenary celebration by Belfast Home Rulers. Volunteer radicalism was hermetically sealed in the past while the passions and polarisation engendered in the later 1790s lived and breathed. The Irish Yeomanry played a key role in this critical transition which saw ancient antipathies sharpen and re-assert their baleful influence after a period of relative calm. The 'age of reason' had briefly promised a brave new world in Ireland. In the 1780s, radical Volunteers favoured Catholic relief along with parliamentary reform. The Boyne Societies, founded to perpetuate the Williamite cause, charged toasting glasses rather than muskets. However the prospect of revolutionary change proved too much to swallow.

The force raised in 1796 actually bore much more resemblance to the Volunteers, praised by United Irish writers such as Myles Byrne and Charles Teeling, than to the reactionary and bigoted organisation portrayed in their rebellion histories. In reality, loyalism in 1796 was still a relatively broad church containing an ideological diversity and fluidity reminiscent of Volunteering days. Indeed, the Yeomanry were largely based on the same membership constituency, with frequent continuity of individual or family service. They certainly included the Williamite tradition found in some Volunteer corps but it also encompassed much of the democratic and indeed radical volunteering spirit. Election of officers was common everywhere. Dublin Yeomen, whom Henry Joy McCracken thought 'liberal', also elected their captains despite governmental opposition. Even in Armagh, the cockpit of Orangeism, Yeomen varied from Diamond veterans in the Crowhill infantry to radical ex-Volunteers enrolled by Lord Charlemont despite quibbles over the oath and the inclusion of some erstwhile francophiles who had recently erected a liberty tree.

In 1796, there was no inconsistency about this. Grattan dubbed the Yeomanry 'an ascendancy army' but in reality the United Irishmen were in the ascendant while the loyalist response was fragmented and in danger of being overwhelmed. The initial priority was defence: to trawl in all varieties of loyalty and provide a structure to prevent people being neutralised or becoming United Irishmen.

The new Yeomanry was therefore a surprisingly diverse force, given their subsequent reputation. The government denied any intention of excluding Catholics or Presbyterians but the system already had the potential for denominational and ideological filtering. Being a Yeoman was a desirable position conveying social status plus pay, clothing, arms and training. Applications exceeded places, which were limited by financial and security considerations. This meant selection locally and government reliance on local landowners' judgement.

Sometimes recruits had no choice. In some areas only Protestants volunteered, in others the Catholic Committee sabotaged Catholic enlistment. In Loughinsholin in County Londonderry, where Presbyterians offered to enlist, Catholics withdrew, and vice-versa. Where there was competition to enter a limited number of corps, choices were unavoidable. Lord Downshire allowed Catholics in his cavalry but faced mutually exclusive Protestant and Catholic infantry offers from the same parishes and opted for the former. In Orange areas, some landowners deliberately selected their Yeomen directly

Flag of the Lower Iveagh Yeoman Cavalry. (Ulster Museum)

from the local lodge. Occasionally a precarious balance was attempted by including proportions of Catholic, Protestant and Dissenter. The Farney corps in County Monaghan started this way. However the first levy produced a predominantly Anglican force. There were Presbyterian Yeomen in mid-Ulster but the strength of the United Irishmen in eastern counties meant relatively few corps were raised there in 1796.

Wealthy, property-owning Catholics, on the other hand, were admitted into cavalry corps. There was an element of tokenism in this: Yeomanry offers of service sometimes highlighted Catholic members, which they never did for the Protestant denominations. In this way it can be estimated that at the very least ten per cent of the first national levy of 20,000 Yeomen were Catholic, thus outnumbering the Orange yeomen who in 1796 were only to be found in some corps in the Orange districts of mid-Ulster.

Forming a Yeomanry force in the deteriorating conditions of 1796 gave the initiative briefly back to Dublin Castle but this disappeared in the crisis following the Bantry Bay invasion attempt. The United Irishmen drew great encouragement from its near success and felt themselves strong enough to switch their policy on the Yeomanry from intimidation to infiltration. As a response, purges of Yeomanry corps began in Ulster and Leinster in the spring of 1797.

Many Catholics were expelled from corps in Wicklow and Wexford on suspicion of being 'United'. In mid-Ulster General John Knox devised a 'test oath' obliging Yeomen to publicly swear they were not United Irishmen. This got results and several corps were cleared of disaffected members. The Presbyterian secretary of the Farney corps was expelled following his confession of United Irish membership while Catholics were removed on the pretext of a political resolution they had issued. Knox followed up the expulsions by permitting augmentations of Orangemen into some northern corps. Although Orangemen quietly joined some corps in 1796 this was the first time they had official approval.

Knox clinched this by engineering Orange resolutions for Castle consumption. This was a risky strategy, given the recent disturbances in Armagh. Knox, a correspondent of the radical MP Arthur O'Connor, privately disapproved of Orangeism but believed the dangerous predicament he faced merited utilising it as a short-term expedient. However, with the United Irish-Defender alliance growing, the precedent inherent in this strategy would have profound and lasting consequences. Almost immediately, symptoms of polarisation appeared. A Tyrone clergyman noted approvingly, 'Our parties are all obviously merged into two: loyalists and traitors'.

However the critical Yeomanry-Orange connection was still to come. By 1798 Orangeism had been adopted by many northern gentry and spread to Dublin where a framework national organisation was established. As insurrection loomed, this provided a ready-made supply of loyal manpower. There were around 18,000 Yeomen in Ulster whereas the Orangemen were conservatively reckoned at 40,000. In March the Dublin leaders offered the Ulster Orangemen to the government if it would arm them. The viceroy, Lord Camden, was scared of offending Catholics in the Militia and hestitated. However, the appointment of an Irishman—Lord Castlereagh—as acting chief secretary offered a solution. On 16 April 1798 he ordered northern Yeomanry commanders to organise 5,000 'supplementary' men to be armed in an emergency. Camden and Castlereagh had privately decided that, where possible, these would be Orangemen.

In tandem with the supplementary plan, regular Yeomen were given a more military role. They were put on permanent duty and integrated into contingency plans for garrisoning key towns at the outbreak of trouble. This had one very important side-effect. In the cramped conditions of garrison life and the panic occasioned by the influx of rural loyalists, Orangeism spread like wildfire amongst both Yeomanry and regular units. This spontaneous, ground-level spread of Orangeism operated simultaneously with Castlereagh's secret emergency policy to utilise Orange manpower in Ulster. The Yeomanry system proved the ideal facilitator for both.

Drum of the Aughnahoe [County Tyrone] Yeoman Infantry. (Ulster Museum)

On 1 July 1798 in the Presbyterian town of Belfast, once the epicentre of United Irish activity, it was noted that 'Every man...has a red coat on'. This would have been inconceivable in 1796 when there was great difficulty enlisting Yeomen. However, it was now government policy to separate northern Presbyterians from the United Irishmen. Again the Yeomanry played a key role. Castlereagh admitted privately that the arrest of the Down United colonel, William Steel Dickson was an exception to 'the policy of acting against the Catholick [sic] rather than the Presbyterian members of the union [United Irishmen]'. Government supporters industriously spread news of the Scullabogue massacre (discussed by Daniel Gahan below) to stir up atavistic fears. The Yeomanry was expanded considerably to meet the emergency and ex-radicals were no longer discouraged. In effect, the Yeomanry functioned as a safety net. Joining up offered an acceptable and very public 'way back' for wavering radicals. Although there were some Presbyterian Yeomen in 1796, many more joined in mid-1798. Charlemont's friend, the Anglican clergyman Edward Hudson, exploited a 'schism' between Presbyterian and Catholic to enlist the former in his Portglenone corps, sardonically noting 'the brotherhood of affection is over'. By 1799, he claimed 'the word "Protestant", which was becoming obsolete in the north, has regained its influence and all of that description seem drawing closer together'. Thus the Yeomanry oath was often a rite of passage for Presbyterians keen to end their flirtation with revolution.

The 1798 rebellion had a profound impact on the psyche of Protestant Ireland, conjuring up anew spectres of the 1641 rebellion. When news of the rising hit Dublin, Camden described the apocalyptic atmosphere to Pitt. The rebellion 'literally made the Protestant part of this country mad...it is scarcely possible to restrain the violence of my own immediate friends and advisors...they are prepared for extirpation and any appearance of lenity...raises a flame which runs like wildfire thro' the streets'. Mercy was indeed scarce until Cornwallis replaced Camden and the rebellion was effectively crushed. Up to this juncture, the interests of most Protestants and the government were running parallel, a partnership potently symbolised by the Yeomanry, now blooded in the rebellion. Many embattled Protestants saw the parallel interests as identical: through the smouldering fires of rebellion they confused expediency with permanent policy.

Cornwallis, a professional soldier, voiced his contempt for the barbarity of the local amateur forces, particularly the Yeomanry. For many, criticism of the Yeomanry was construed as attacking Protestant interests. Yeomanry service under Camden and the relationship it represented was now seen as an unalterable 'gold standard'. When government policy ran counter to perceived Protestant interests, loyalty was qualified with distrust and a feeling of betrayal. Camden was toasted as 'the father of the Yeomanry' while Cornwallis was lampooned as 'Croppywallis'.

When it emerged that Prime Minister Pitt intended legislative union, antagonism towards Cornwallis sharpened. As union would remove emancipation from Ireland's control, ultra-Protestant loyalty faced a severe test. Many Yeomen and Orangemen opposed the measure, particularly in Dublin where lawyers and merchants also faced a loss of professional and mercantile status. The Yeomanry, which it was claimed saved Ireland in 1798, were at the cutting edge of the anti-union campaign. A mutiny was threatened in Dublin with Volunteer-type rhetoric, but the bluster of 1782 proved hot air in post-rebellion Ireland. In the last analysis Protestants depended on the Yeomanry and the Yeomen depended on the government. The consequences of disbandment made union seem the lesser evil. Cornwallis rushed reinforcements to Dublin but the bluff had called itself.

Jonah Barrington later claimed the Volunteers were loyal to their country [Ireland] and their king while the Yeomen looked to 'the king of England and his ministers'. Barrington's jibe about patriotism was the peevish reaction of an incorrigible anti-unionist, yet a subtle alteration in the nature and focus of loyalty had occurred. The Volunteers' 'patriotism' flourished in an atmosphere where they faced no real internal threat. While many Yeomen opposed the abolition of the Irish parliament, the experience of 1798 made challenging the executive a luxury they could not afford. On the surface, the switch of loyalty from College Green to Dublin Castle seemed relatively smooth: Yeomanry corps quickly adopted the post-1800 union flag in their colours. Yet, alongside this, a new focus of loyalty emerged to co-exist with this sometimes grudging allegiance. The 'Protestant nationalism' of 1782 was transformed into a clenching loyalty to the increasingly insecure interests of Irish Protestants.

The Yeomanry soon became a major component in post-union politics, a conduit between government and substantial numbers of Protestants who increasingly saw the force as symbolising the survival of their social and political position. They functioned as a political tool. When Hardwicke, the new viceroy, wanted to send a conciliatory message to nervous Protestants he reviewed the entire Dublin Yeomanry in Phoenix Park, then lavished hospitality on the officers in a banquet afterwards. It was a two-way process: Protestants could use the Yeomanry to put government in their debt. The continuance of war in 1803 meant a large increase in the Yeomanry from 63,000 to around 80,000. Emmet's rising, coming when this augmentation was on foot, gave Protestants another opportunity to appear indispensable by extending their monopoly of the Yeomanry. The means by which this was accomplished ranged from high-level manoeuvring to parish pump politics.

As a partisan Yeomanry would be viewed in a poor light at Westminster, Hardwicke attempted a balance by considering some purely Catholic corps. However the Louth MP Chichester Fortesque threatened impeachment if he proceeded. Even the chief secretary, William Wickham, considered Catholic corps 'unsafe' as they would inflame loyalist opinion and 'be not cried but roared out against throughout all Ireland'. At a local level, Arthur Browne, the Prime Sergeant of Limerick, observed that Yeomanry corps in each town he passed on circuit effectively excluded Catholics by submitting prospective recruits to a ballot of existing members. This said, the Protestant monopoly was never total. Catholic Yeomen remained in areas of sparse Protestant settlement like Kerry. Moreover, there was still a scattering of liberal Protestants, usually at officer level, like Lieutenant Barnes of the Armagh Yeomanry. However, the general tendency was clear. When it became known Barnes had signed an emancipation petition, the privates mutinied and flung down their arms.

In the early nineteenth century, the passions generated by 1798 mixed with the politics of the Catholic Question. The continued existence of the Yeomanry allowed Protestants to demonstrate that their traditional control of law and order was intact as the campaign for emancipation built up. Yeomanry parades and the use of the force in assisting magistrates with mundane law and order matters assumed great symbolic importance as tangible manifestations of the fractures in Irish society. Yeomanry corps inevitably became involved in local clashes in an increasingly sectarianised atmosphere. In 1807, the government prevented Enniscorthy Yeomen celebrating the anniversary of the battle of Vinegar Hill as it raised sectarian tensions. In 1808 Yeomen were among a mob which disrupted a St John's Eve bonfire and 'garland' near Newry, provoking a riot in which one man died. During the disturbances which swept Kerry and Limerick the same year, isolated Protestant Yeomen were singled out for attacks and arms raids. Since penal times, possession or dispossession of arms scored political points. Protestant insecurity and Catholic alienation fed off each other. O'Connell, ironically once a Yeoman himself, upped the ante by lambasting the force as symbolising a partisan magistracy.

The Yeomanry presented governments with a dilemma: was their strategic utility worth the political price? While war with France continued and the regular army was depleted for overseas service, they provided an important source of additional manpower and were particularly useful during invasion scares when they could free up the remaining regular garrison and maintain a local presence to deter co-ordinated action by the disaffected. Moreover, they served an unofficial purpose by keeping potentially turbulent Protestants under discipline.

The decision was deferred and the dilemma submerged. For much of the 1820s the Yeomanry lingered on, a rather moribund force seen by officials as a liability which could not be disbanded for fear of a Protestant reaction, particularly in Ulster where the force was numerically strongest. The advent of the denominationally inclusive County Constabulary in 1822 further touched Protestant insecurity by removing much of the functional justification for Yeomanry. There was no love lost between the two forces. In 1830 William McMullan of the Lurgan infantry was arrested by his own captain, yelling at the head of a mob rioting against the police, 'we have plenty of arms and ammunition and can use them as well as you'. Ironically in that year the Whig chief secretary, Stanley, had decided to re-clothe and re-arm the Yeomanry as part of the response to the southern Tithe War. Stanley's experiment proved disastrous as sectarian clashes developed.

In some districts the sight of a red coat was like a red rag to a bull. In 1831, the rescue of two heifers destrained for tithe sparked an appalling incident in Newtownbarry. A mob of locals tried to release the cattle, the magistrates called for Yeomanry and stones were thrown. When one Yeoman fell with a fractured skull, the others opened fire killing fourteen countrymen. The viceroy, Anglesey, tried to limit the political damage by initiating a progressive dismantling of the Yeomanry starting with a stand-down of the permanent sergeants which meant the Yeomen could no longer drill. This phasing-out took three years and was intentionally gradual, starving the Yeomanry of the oxygen of duty and pay, thus letting them pass away naturally if not gracefully. It was rightly felt this approach would be less likely to provoke a political reaction than sudden disbandment which, for a Protestant community coming to terms with emancipation, would have been like an amputation without anaesthetic.

Although the Yeomanry's official existence ended in 1834, the last rusty muskets were not removed from their dusty stores till the early 1840s. With unintentional but obvious symbolism, they were escorted to the ordnance stores by members of the new constabulary. Although gone, the Yeomen were most certainly not forgotten. For one thing, they were seen as the most recent manifestation of a tradition of Protestant self-defence stretching back to plantation requirements of armed service from tenants then re-surfacing in different forms such as the Williamite county associations, the eighteenth-century Boyne Societies, anti-Jacobite associations of 1745 and the Volunteers. Such identification had been eagerly promoted. At the foundation of an Apprentice Boys' club in 1813, Colonel Blacker, a Yeoman and Orangeman, amalgamated the siege tradition, the Yeomanry and 1798 in a song entitled *The Crimson Banner*:

> Again when treason maddened round,
>
> and rebel hordes were swarming,
>
> were Derry's sons the foremost found,
>
> for King and Country arming.

Moreover, the idea of a yeomanry remained as a structural template for local, gentry-led self-defence, particularly in Ulster. When volunteering was revived in Britain in 1859, northern Irish MPs like Sharman Crawford tried unsuccessfully to use the Yeomanry precedent to get similar Irish legislation. Yeomanry-like associations were mooted in the second Home Rule crisis of 1893. The Ulster Volunteer Force of 1911-14—often led by the same families like Knox of Dungannon—defined their role like Yeomen, giving priority to local defence and exhibiting great reluctance to leave their own districts for training in brigades.

The strong Orange-Yeomanry connection—itself part of a wider process of militarisation in Irish society—has left an enduring imprint on Orangeism which can be seen in the marching fife and drum bands and in various military regalia such as ceremonial swords and pikes. Even the name is still retained by the Moira Yeomanry Loyal Orange Lodge. The town or parish basis of

Yeomanry corps mirrored the dynamics of the plantations and helped catapult the territorial mind-set of both 'planter' and 'native' into the nineteenth century and beyond. Weekly Yeomanry parades defined territory in the same way as rural drumming parties in the nineteenth century and marches, murals and coloured kerbstones in the twentieth.

Chapter Nine

The military strategy of the Wexford United Irishmen in 1798

Daniel Gahan

Until the 1990s historians of 1798 regarded the rebellion in Wexford as a spontaneous popular reaction to unwarranted government repression and not part of a larger United Irish conspiracy. Scanty references to the county in the manuscript record and the bitter, apparently localised, character of the Wexford conflict seemed to support this interpretation.

Now, inspired by the pioneering work of Louis Cullen, historians look at the Wexford rising very differently. They point out that Wexford political life was sophisticated in the 1790s and that there was an elaborate United Irish network in the county on the eve of the insurrection, thereby discrediting explanations which suggest that Wexford people rose up simply to avoid being slaughtered by a cruel government.

Examining the military conduct of the Wexford United Irishmen in the light of this new interpretation, the strategy adopted by the rebel leadership begins to make sense. The Wexford rebels set out to attain specified military goals. When they achieved these (and they did so efficiently and thoroughly) their task was all but completed. Their comrades in other counties did not match their success however; as a result they found themselves initially confused and, ultimately isolated. This turn of events, and not a fondness for drink or a failure to impose discipline, explains many of the moves they made in the last three weeks of their struggle and it may also explain the tragic episodes which occurred as their cause began to collapse.

The particular tasks facing the Wexford United Irishmen are well understood. Their job was to mobilise first at local and then at county-wide level and to ensure that all government forces inside the county were either destroyed or tied down. In the meantime the epicentre of the rising would be in Dublin City which was to be seized from within by local units (In the event, on the evening of 23 May, this part of the plan was pre-empted by the rapid mobilisation of the city's Yeomanry at the intended rebel rendezvous points). At the same time

United Irishmen from the counties immediately adjacent (Dublin, Meath, Kildare and Wicklow) were first to form a cordon of positions around the city (thus isolating it from possible government reinforcement) and then to advance on it in order to reinforce their comrades within (In the event only the first objective was accomplished). United Irish forces beyond (including those in Wexford) were to seize control of their own counties but were not expected to join in offensive action outside of them.

The pattern of initial United Irish mobilisation in Wexford fits this model very well. Louis Cullen demonstrated that by mid-May 1798 the United Irishmen were well organised in County Wexford, especially in northern and central parishes, and were establishing themselves in the south. His evidence for this was the geographical distribution of United Irish officers, identified as colonels and captains, as well as the actual mobilisation in the early hours and days of the rising in those areas to which he paid close attention - the parishes east and west of Eniscorthy.

If we take Cullen's work as our point of departure and look at mobilisation in the county at large, we discover a pattern that confirms almost everything in his analysis. Thus, a survey of surviving contemporary accounts suggests that initial mobilisation took place on the night of 26-27 May, in a wide crescent of parishes from near Newtownbarry, on the border with Carlow, to Oulart and Blackwater on the county's east coast, a distance of over twenty-five miles. The signal for this mobilisation was the arrival of news of the midland rising that afternoon. The actual process was the same in all parts of this crescent: under cover of darkness, bands of men, usually twenty or thirty to each unit, gathered at pre-arranged meeting places and then converged on more important assembly points. By noon the next day, particularly large numbers had massed at Kilthomas and Oulart, at either end of that crescent. It had all the hallmarks of a well-planned operation; when examined closely it shows few signs of being a spontaneous popular response to a 'great fear'. The failure of the rebels around Gorey to join in at this stage can be readily explained by the fact that their colonel, Anthony Perry of Inch, had been taken prisoner and tortured by the authorities a few days beforehand and was not able to co-ordinate the movement there for the time being.

The diffusion of the rising from this initial crescent was rapid and shows signs of having been equally well orchestrated. On 28 May, the rebels who had massed at Oulart the day before, swung around to the north of Eniscorthy and combined with the Kilthomas group at Scarawalsh and with other units from parishes to the west of the Slaney at Ballyorrill Hill. Then the combined force marched on the town in a fashion that suggests co-ordination not spontaneity.

The Battle of Ballyellis. (National Library of Ireland)

Rebel units to the west and south-west of Enniscorthy were already mobilising by the evening of 28 May; they joined the main camp on Vinegar Hill the following day, as did numerous bands from the north Wexford/south Wicklow borderlands. By the night of 29 May therefore, rebel units had mobilised in and seized almost every parish in the northern two-thirds of the county, the district around Gorey being the only possible exception (We might note here that there was a debate among the leaders on Vinegar Hill that afternoon as to whether they should attack New Ross or Wexford town next and in the end they chose to attack the latter. Significantly though, they gave little consideration to an attack on Gorey at this stage, suggesting that they assumed their well-organised comrades in Carlow and Wicklow would neutralise the government threat from that quarter).

Late on 29 May the now huge rebel army marched south to Forth Mountain, just outside Wexford town. On the following day, the forth of the rising, they took the town. The garrison slipped away and escaped to Duncannon Fort, depriving them of a valuable chance to acquire arms and ammunition. There are hints in contemporary accounts though that as this was happening, rebel units in the south-east and south-west of the county were already forming. So, for example, local rebels may have launched a small and ineffective ambush against the fleeing garrison at Mayglass, to the south of the town that morning; by the following morning an army of two thousand men was ready to march into the county capital from parishes to its south. Additionally, a rebel unit from Loughnageer almost certainly conducted an ambush at Taylorstown Bridge,

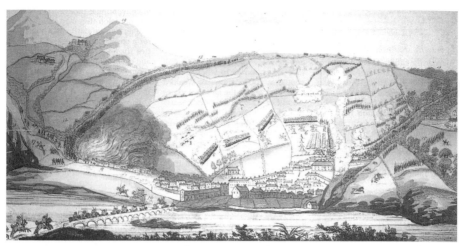

Contemporary print of the battle of Arklow (Kevin Whelan)

in Shelburne barony later that night. Clearly, the rebellion spread into the far south-east and far south-west of the county both *before* government forces drove the people to rebel by their atrocities and *before* insurgent armies had the chance to intimidate people into joining.

An extraordinary situation had developed in County Wexford by the end of the fourth day of rebellion, 30 May. The insurgents had driven government forces from the entire county, with the exception of footholds at Duncannon, New Ross, Newtownbarry and Gorey; only the Gorey garrison was any distance within the county boundary. They had done so in a lightening campaign in which they had not once relaxed the pressure on their enemies and had demonstrated the ability to adopt unconventional tactics (On at least one occasion they had used a stampeding herd of cattle as a substitute for a cavalry charge and in their battles they relied heavily on the pike and close combat). On the whole, the campaign shows every sign of having been well planned, and to have been limited in its strategic objectives.

The steps the rebels took the next day, 31 May, make perfect sense if we assume that they saw themselves as only a peripheral part of a nationwide uprising, complementing a decisive seizure of the capital, Dublin. First, they selected Bagenal Harvey as their commander-in-chief but with very little real power. This was befitting a post assumed to be temporary pending more specific instructions from the United Irish leadership in Dublin. Second, rather than keeping their forces united and driving out into Munster or the midlands and thereby spreading the rebellion, they divided them into three separate divisions, each with the objective of reducing a particular government foothold. This too

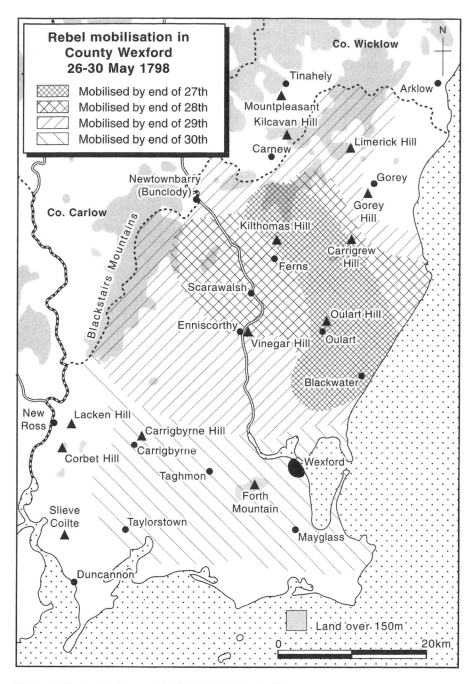

Rebel mobilisation in County Wexford 26–30 May 1798

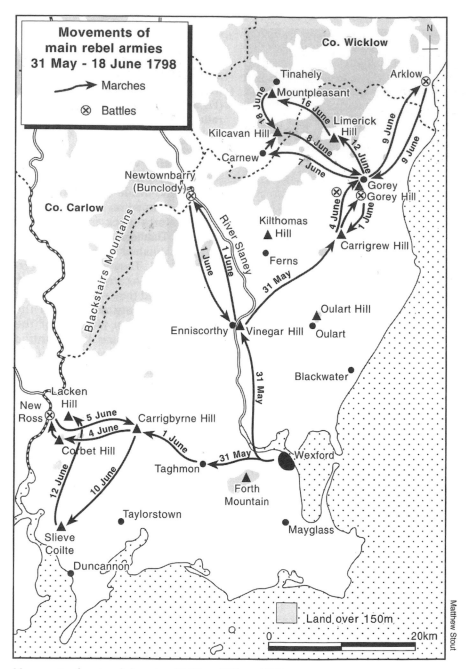

Movements of main rebel armies, 31 May–18 June 1798

is consistent with a limited strategy of rounding out the liberation of their own county but not pushing beyond its boundaries.

Decisiveness characterised the next twenty-four hours of the Wexford rising too. By nightfall on 31 May, one division was back at Vinegar Hill, poised to attack Newtownbarry the next morning, another was at Carrigrew, ready to move against Gorey, and a third, the division under Harvey himself, was at Taghmon, ready to move on New Ross.

All this changed dramatically the following day, 1 June, the sixth day of the rising, and in many respects its most critical turning point. On this day the rebels began to realise that something had gone badly wrong with the rebellion elsewhere in the country. Initially, the evidence was probably vague and confusing but as the days passed it must have become clearer to them. On that day, the divisions sent to attack Newtownbarry and Gorey both ran into unexpectedly stout resistance and were driven back with heavy losses to their camps at Vinegar Hill and Carrigrew. The division headed for New Ross got as far as Carrickbyrne by evening but did not launch their attack as yet. On the following day, 2 June, with word of defeats further north filtering southward, rebel boats outside Wexford harbour captured Lord Kingsborough, commander of the North Cork Militia. Since he had left Dublin after the rising had failed there, he almost certainly passed on the news to rebel leaders in the town, and it may have begun to filter out to rebel camps in other parts of the county soon afterwards. Kingsborough would have known little about the midland rebellion at this point and could not have given then accurate information on Ulster either. Even if the Wexford leaders assumed that all was well with their midland and Ulster comrades the news of a Dublin collapse would have been a severe blow to their hopes. Having already been informed of the defeats at Newtownbarry and Gorey, it must have given them real reason to doubt their chances of success.

Their actions from this point on are a curious mixture of extreme caution and desperate boldness which betray the anxiety that was beginning to creep into their ranks. So, for example, on 2 and 3 June, the rebels camped at Carrickbyrne and Carrigrew marked time drilling and waiting, probably because they were unsure of what to do next. Then, between 4 and 9 June they suddenly mounted offensives against the government toeholds on the perimeter of the county that betrayed all the hallmarks of both confusion and desperation. First was the disastrous attack on New Ross by the southern division on 5 June, followed by attacks by the northern division on the towns of Carnew on 7 June and Arklow on 9 June; the first was a success, the second a failure. These offensives against New Ross and Arklow came after days of hesitation while their garrisons were being reinforced by the government. Thus the southerners remained immobilised at Carrickbyrne for three days in all before attacking New Ross; the northerners, who had reached Gorey Hill (after a morale-boosting skirmish at Tubberneering) on the 4th, did not move against Arklow for five days.

The rebel response to this series of setbacks was perfectly sensible - given their assumption that the issue was still being decided elsewhere and that Dublin might yet be cut off by rebels from the midlands (a few days previously such a plan was communicated to the Wexford rebels by the United Irish envy, Father John Martin of Drogheda) - they simply bided their time. So, we find that in the southern part of the county the rebel forces passed the entire two week period between 6 and 19 June deploying from hilltop to hilltop but making no attempt to launch another attack on New Ross. They spent two days on Carrickbyrne, moved atop Slievecoilte for one or two days and then marched north to Lacken Hill and remained there, just two miles from New Ross, for an entire week. Similarly, their northern comrades passed the two days immediately following the battle of Arklow on Gorey Hill; they then went to Limerick Hill, where they remained for four or five days; then they pushed just inside the Wicklow border and camped on Mountpleasant; finally, after a quick and successful attack on Tinahely, they turned south and established themselves on Kilcavan Hill. They made few determined efforts to carry the fight to the enemy nor did they attempt to break out of the county and spread the rebellion into east Munster or the midlands, something they (or the southern division) could surely have accomplished had they so wished (The remarkable treks by rebel remnants into the heart of the midlands in the aftermath of the defeat at Vinegar Hill on 21 June is proof of this).

The outpouring of scholarship on the United Irish movement from the 1980s on threw a great deal of light on the various components of the 1798 Rebellion. Modern research demolishes the myth of the rebels as a rural mob, perpetuated initially by Richard Musgrave and other loyalist commentators but inadvertently supported by former rebels anxious to conceal the extent of their involvement in an elaborate conspiracy to overthrow a government by force of arms, and given a new lease of life by Thomas Pakenham's *The Year of Liberty* (1969) whose rebel divisions were brave but fanatical and undisciplined mobs. In fact, the Wexford rebels were politically and militarily far more sophisticated than these accounts would have us believe.

Chapter Ten

The Scullabogue massacre, 1798

Daniel Gahan

Few events in modern Irish history, especially in the history of revolutionary nationalism, haunt the imagination like the massacre that took place in the townland of Scullabogue in southern County Wexford on 5 June 1798. The killing of well over a hundred government supporters by rebels has been immortalised in the illustration that George Cruickshank produced for William Maxwell's narrative of the rebellion, published in the middle of the last century. This, along with the vivid descriptions of many later historians, have immortalised the event in the Irish historical consciousness.

The massacre occurred in a farmstead that was located at the foot of Carrickbyrne Hill, the main campsite of the southern division of the Wexford rebel army in the early days of the insurrection. The main body of that army had gone six miles to the west the evening before, to attack the town of New Ross, and had left a guarding party in charge of their loyalist prisoners. The next morning, as the battle for New Ross raged between government and rebel forces, they hauled close to forty men out of the dwelling house of the farmstead and shot them, four at a time, on the lawn. At the same time, other rebels attacked a larger group of prisoners being held in other parts of the farm and drove them into a large barn; there they shot at them and piked them until some of the prisoners slammed shut the barn doors. Then the guards set the building on fire. Inside, panic broke out. Between trampling, smoke and flames, all of those in the building died. The victims included men of all ages, a number of women, and several children. Most of them were Protestants, although around twenty are claimed to have been Catholics. There were many atrocities that summer, perpetrated by both sides, but none can match Scullabogue in terms of raw brutality. It was the single largest case of mass murder, by either side, and, very significantly, it was the only case in which rebels killed women and children. Beyond that, it was the only major atrocity associated with Wexford rebels from the area to the south of the Slaney. In more than one way then, it stands out as a kind of grim aberration.

Efforts to reconstruct the circumstances surrounding the massacre and to detail the killings themselves are hampered by lack of evidence. Eyewitness accounts of the massacre are few. A number of depositions, taken from the relatives of victims, were transcribed by Sir Richard Musgrave and published three years after the event, and these give us some insight. In addition, the records of several of the court martial trials of individuals accused of having taken part have survived. We also have the very vivid accounts of the event on the loyalist side written by Sir Richard Musgrave and George Taylor. Both accounts appeared in its immediate aftermath and both are based on evidence collected from those indirectly familiar with it. On the 'pro-rebel' side we have the memoirs of Edward Hay and Thomas Cloney. Neither was present at the killings either but Hay travelled the county in the year or so after the rising and talked to those generally familiar with it, Scullabogue included. Cloney spent the day of the battle in New Ross, where he took a prominent part in the fighting, and returned to Carrickbyrne the next morning. His account is chiefly valuable for the details it provides of the battle. Most critical of all is the very detailed narrative of the battle of New Ross compiled by James Alexander, a former officer in the British army and a seemingly fair-minded observer. His version of events, more than any other, has a genuine ring of truth about it; he was a loyalist, tried and true, but it is clear that he also disapproved strongly of the abuses to which soldiers in the New Ross garrison resorted before, during and after the battle.

What then were the circumstances surrounding the massacre and what does the context of the event tell us about why it may have taken place? The first thing we must note here is that the creation of a makeshift prison camp at Scullabogue was in itself not unusual. It was common for rebel divisions, once they established themselves at a strong-point, to send parties out into the surrounding countryside to round up people they suspected of pro-government sympathies. This happened in the area around Enniscorthy and it also took place in and around Wexford town and Gorey. Those rounded up were mostly Protestants, although some Catholics were held too. While there may have been a sectarian undertone to the process everywhere, it is noteworthy that some of the rebel officers who ordered these sweeps and some of the rank-and-file who took part in them were themselves Protestants. In most places those seized were not initially harmed, although the rebel units based on Vinegar Hill executed several men each day (usually two or three a day), over the course of the four weeks they held the county. These killings normally followed a period of incarceration in a brewery at the foot of the hill and a trial at its summit. There were eventually killings at Gorey and Wexford town too, but they took place in the final days of the rebel regime when panic had invaded their ranks and

George Cruikshank's depiction of the massacre at Scullabogue, from W.H. Maxwell, History of the Irish rebellion of 1798 (1845)

when internal factional struggles caused imprisoned government supporters to be sacrificed.

The process of rounding up prisoners in the vicinity of Carrickbyrne Hill followed roughly the same pattern as elsewhere. The rebels established a camp there on 1 June, in preparation for their anticipated attack on New Ross, and over the next two days small parties went out into nearby townlands and villages and arrested well over a hundred people. Most of those taken came from inside a triangular area stretching from Foulkesmills to Adamstown to Fethard, that is, from the areas to the north, south and east of the camp. The fact that loyalist families in townlands to the west of the hill had had time to escape to New Ross before the rebels arrived in the area probably explains why so few of them were picked up.

The rebels who conducted the arrests were mostly from the locality in which they were operating and knew well those they had taken to the prison camp. We have the names of thirty-two individuals who carried out the sweeps. They came from a widely scattered area around the camp but an usually large number came from the townland of Kilbride, just north of Fethard. A significant number also came from the villages of Saltmills, Fethard and Tintern. Most seem to have been tenant farmers, although there was a scattering of labourers and artisans among them too.

Three rebels were especially prominent in the round-up and they represent something of a cross-section of the rebel officership in this part of the county. The most important of them was Michael Devereux of Battlestown, a townland about three miles west of the campsite. He led rebel parties to the villages of Tintern and Fethard on at least three occasions over those early June days. He was part of the larger Devereux connection, descended from 'Old English' landlords who had lost their estates in the seventeenth century. In 1798 his family still held the entire townland of Battlestown, about six hundred acres, and, remarkably, still held it in 1810, even though he was transported for his part in the rebellion. As a member of the Catholic middleman class of south Wexford, Devereux is typical of the rebel officer corps from that part of the county and his involvement in the round-up of suspected government supporters is not surprising.

Even more interesting are Joshua Colfer of Fethard village, a maltster, and a John Houghron of the village of Tintern, a stone mason. The evidence of the depositions suggests that these two men led rebel search parties also and came through their home villages several times looking for suspects. Significantly, among those arrested and harassed by Colfer was the Clarke family of Fethard, his former employers. For his part Houghran operated mostly in and around Tintern and those who were prominent in his party included a tailor and a labourer.

The social status of rebels involved in the round-up may be quite significant. Much of south-west Wexford was in the hands of only a few large landlords. Two of these, the Loftus and Tottenham families, were closely associated with the conservative cause in the politics of the 1790s, while the other two, the Colcloughs and Leighs, had once been Catholic and were still associated with the liberal side of local politics. Tenant farmers are almost certain to have been drawn into the maelstrom of the liberal/conservative struggle in such an area. To add to a very tense and highly politicised situation, three small Protestant colonies had been established in the villages of Tintern, Old Ross and Fethard earlier in the eighteenth century and these had remained very prominent pro-ascendancy enclaves up to the 1790s; this was especially true of the Old Ross settlement which was an exclusively Palatine Protestant community, located on a small tract of land owned by the Rams of Gorey, a steadfastly pro-ascendancy family. If we consider the political and sectarian symbolism of such communities, and the likelihood that economic rivalry surely developed between craftsmen and labourers of both religions in their vicinity, then it is not surprising that Catholic artisans and labourers would be active in the campaign against such people. Added to any radical or revolutionary agenda, in other words, was a local social and sectarian agenda, fuelled in large part by economic rivalries.

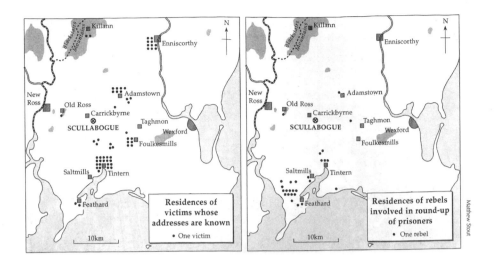

The more immediate circumstances of the massacre are confusing but the fragments of evidence available allow us to untangle them to some extent. Perhaps the most important thing about it is its connection to the battle of New Ross, only six miles away. The rebel attack on the town came at sunrise, 4.05 am, according to the official calendar of 1798. According to Alexander's account fighting reached into the heart of the town by six or seven o'clock. Government troops conducted the first of several counter-attacks in the next hour or two, possibly as early as eight o'clock but certainly by nine.

During these attacks (and there is ample evidence from Alexander to support this), soldiers took to systematically killing captured and wounded rebels. This was not unique to them, as both rebel and government forces had done so before but, in the middle of this indiscriminate slaughter, one group of soldiers surrounded and set fire to a large house in Mary Street in which about seventy wounded rebels were lying. They prevented all but one man from escaping and Alexander claimed the screams of the terrified doomed men could be clearly heard, despite the noise of the battle, over much of the town.

The issue of timing is critical here. The only witness who specifies the time at which the massacre began in Scullabogue, places it at between nine and ten o' clock that morning. If the burning of the house in New Ross took place as early as 8.30 am or even as late as 9.30 am, there was ample time for an incensed rebel to ride eastwards to Scullabogue with orders to kill all the prisoners, justifying this by an appeal to what had just taken place in the streets of New Ross. The only men in a position to recount what happened in the hours before the massacre began that morning, Cloney and Hay, strongly suggest that Bagenal

Harvey and the other rebel commanders had no connection to the event and even most loyalist historians seem to concur with this. The consensus instead is that retreating rebel units carried back the instruction to kill the prisoners and that the order came from somewhere other than the rebel commanders. The commander of the guarding party was a Captain John Murphy of Loughnageer, a nearby townland. He apparently refused early instructions to kill the prisoners, but eventually, after messengers had come from the direction of New Ross with orders to put them all to death for the third time, he agreed and told his men to proceed.

What happened once the order was given is not quite clear either. From the evidence we have though we can assert with some confidence that the kind of frantic mob scene depicted in Cruickshank's illustration did not occur. Instead, it appears that around twenty or so rebels conducted the entire massacre while most of the guarding party stood about and watched. The killings were not carried out hurriedly, therefore, but were conducted in a chillingly methodical fashion; this is especially true of the executions on the lawn in front of the farmhouse.

Most of the men who actually did the killing can be identified, and a profile of the group suggests some surprising features. Of the seventeen rank-and-file rebels which the depositions link directly to the slaughter, three, John Ellard, Robert Mills and John Turner, were Protestants; all three later claimed that they acted out of fear for their own lives (a common claim by former rebels in the years afterwards). Mills provided detailed evidence of the activities of those around him at the court martials and seems to have been set free by way of payment for his evidence, this in spite of the fact that he admitted hacking at prisoners trying to escape from the barn with his pike and striking a woman prisoner so hard with the weapon that it bent. Five, Patrick Furlong, Patrick Kerrivan, Michael Quigley, Daniel Sullivan, and John Tobin, were present at the killings, carried weapons at the time but were not actually seen to shoot or pike prisoners or set the barn on fire. Furlong and Sullivan were executed; Quigley and Tobin—who was about sixteen years of age—were transported; the fate of Kerrivan is unknown.

The remaining nine men, along with Robert Mills, were the hard core of the killers. This group consisted of two sets of brothers, John and Thomas Mahony and Nicholas and Thomas Parle. There was also Matthew Furlong (who may or may not have been related to a Matthew Furlong of Templescoby who was among those shot by soldiers in cold blood that morning in New Ross) and John Keefe, James Leary, Mitchell Redmond, and Michael Murphy. All nine were accused of having shot or stabbed prisoners at the door of the barn and three, Furlong, Leary and Murphy, were identified as having set the straw roof of the

The Battle of Ross. by George Cruikshank, from (Maxwell, History of the Irish Rebellion in 1798 Cruikshank was at the height of his fame when he drew the book's technically brilliant illustrations. These heavily propagandist works paved the way for the brutish simian 'Paddy' which was to become the British stereotype of the post-famine period.

barn on fire. All nine were executed, a few in the late summer of 1798 itself, but most in the summer of 1799 and in the spring of 1800.

There were a few other people associated with the incident whose exact role is unclear. One deposition claimed that rebel officers Nicholas Sweetman of Newbawn and Walter Devereux of Taghmon were present. The evidence is not strong but Devereux was alleged to have praised the action later that day. He was captured a few weeks after the rebellion in Cork as he tried to take ship for America; the authorities hurriedly tried and executed him. Even more intriguing is the case of Father Brien Murphy, a suspended priest who lived in Taghmon and who was claimed to have been the one who sent word to kill the prisoners. There is reason to believe that the priest was in fact involved; several sources mention him in this role and even James Gordon, the widely respected Protestant historian of the rebellion, points an accusing finger. Surprisingly, though, Murphy somehow escaped the worst of the counter-revolutionary terror and as late as 1803 we find him asking James Caulfield, the Catholic bishop of Ferns, to believe his promises of good behaviour and to allow him to administer the sacraments. We can only conclude that he went into hiding while the hunt for former rebel officers was underway and came out in the open a year or two later and survived partly because of his connection with the Catholic Church.

What conclusions can we draw from this cursory summary of the evidence? We must first acknowledge that the rounding up of suspected government loyalists was common practice everywhere in Wexford during the rebellion, and the killing of prisoners was not unknown either; in this sense what happened at Scullabogue was part of a larger pattern, albeit on a larger scale and carried out in an especially brutal manner. Beyond this though, the evidence strongly suggests that the killings took place as an immediate reaction to atrocities in the battle of New Ross, raging six miles away. It suggests that they were ordered by what can only be described as renegade officers and carried out hesitantly by only part of the guarding party and not by the entire unit. Finally, while it is undeniable that sectarian hatred had some part to play in the affair, I suspect that as we learn more about the crime and the people who carried it out, it will be seen to fit the larger pattern of social and political violence that was characteristic of Ireland at large and the Atlantic world as a whole in the era of the French Revolution; the sectarian dimension will then come to appear far more incidental to the affair than it has hitherto seemed.

Chapter Eleven

1798 in the north

A.T.Q. Stewart

On 26 May 1798, the very day on which rebellion erupted in Wexford, a despondent Wolfe Tone offered to serve Bonaparte in India. He had just heard the rumour that the Toulon fleet was bound for the East and not for England. Learning some days later that Lord Edward Fitzgerald had been arrested, he recorded that he did not know him very well, but he suspected that the poor fellow had been premeditating an attack on Dublin. His detachment startles us, until we remember why he was in Paris; he naturally regarded any outbreak in Ireland as premature. It was 18 June, and the Wexford rising almost over, before accurate and detailed news of it reached him and his reaction was one of surprise: 'In all this business I do not hear one syllable about the North, which astonishes me more than I can express. Are they afraid? Have they changed their opinions? What can be the cause of their passive submission, at this moment, so little suited to their former zeal and energy?'.

His bewilderment was understandable. For three weeks the sullen torpor which had descended on the North had astounded all Ireland, including Dublin Castle, where Edward Cooke, the Under-Secretary, found it 'unaccountable'. Belfast had, after all, been the radical cradle of the United Irish movement in 1791. It was at first a constitutional pressure group, but when, in the years after the outbreak of war with France, it was succeeded by the 'new system', an underground revolutionary army had been recruited and organised there, waiting only for a French invasion to proclaim a republic. This United Irish army had reached its greatest numerical strength in the summer of 1797, when rebellion had seemed almost certain. Since then it had been slowly declining, though the province of Ulster had been in a state of barely-smothered civil war. When the mail coach signal came on 23 May 1798, the military braced themselves for revolt in the north. Instead it broke out behind their back in Wexford.

General George Nugent, who held the northern command, was a figure far removed from the caricature familiar in Irish accounts of 1798. Urbane and well connected (he was, among other things, MP for Buckingham), Nugent's demeanour was in stark contrast to that of his predecessor, General Lake, the martinet who was now commander-in-chief in Ireland. Lake had held the radicals of Belfast in utter contempt, but Nugent had made a good impression, and thought well enough of the town and its society to have his wedding there. Patient and diplomatic, he managed to negotiate the handing over of four of the old Volunteer cannon taken by the local United Irishmen (the fifth gun was spirited away, to reappear at the battle of Antrim).

This diplomacy paid dividends at a time when the attitude of the Protestant Dissenters was rapidly changing. Some of the most vociferous of the Belfast merchants were deserting the reform cause for economic reasons. Enthusiasm for the French waned when the Revolution degenerated into the Terror, and cooled altogether when the French Republic attacked Holland and Switzerland, and threatened war with the United States. Among the first to draw attention to this altered climate were the clergy of the Church of Ireland. Thomas Percy, bishop of Dromore (more celebrated as the author of the *Reliques of ancient English poetry* (1765)) told his wife: 'A wonderful change has taken place among the republicans of the north, especially in and near Belfast. They now abhor the French as much as they were formerly partial to them, and are grown quite loyal'. Dean Warburton gave it as his opinion that the 'cunning and wary northerners can see no revolution can be effected without foreign aid (of which they now despair)...I think the northern Dissenter will now quietly be a spectator of that destructive flame which he himself originally kindled up, and will take no active part in the present attempt'.

Just over a week later he seemed to be proved wrong. On Thursday 7 June, a day of warm sunshine and cloudless skies, County Antrim rose. Nonetheless, General Nugent had had two precious weeks to prepare for the event. Intelligence was flowing in which enabled him to estimate the extent of the threat; his chief problem was that his resources were being weakened by continual detaching to the south, and promised reinforcements from Scotland and England were slow to arrive. When they did, they were cavalry and it was infantry he needed. Under the surface calm there had been an agonising indecision in what was left of the United Irish leadership. Robert Simms, the Belfast merchant who was the chosen adjutant-general for County Antrim was convinced that rebellion would not succeed without the aid of French arms. Assembling the colonels of the various United Irish regiments was a difficult and perilous business in conditions of martial law and curfew. When they did meet, they could not agree. Simms procrastinated, and, because he could not obtain a consensus, he put off liaising with his opposite number in County Down, the Revd William Steel Dickson, until it was too late. Some of his officers, like James Hope, began to suspect him of treachery. There was considerable doubt about the other

The Battle of Antrim by J.W. Carey, 1895. (Ulster Museum)

counties and a last crisis meeting of the provincial committee held in Armagh on 29 May denounced the leadership and resolved that if the colonels could not agree next day on insurrection they should all return to their occupations and deceive the people no longer.

The fatal thread of indecision ran through all that followed. When the Antrim colonels met at Parkgate on 1 June they were disturbed by a party of dragoons who rode through the village by chance. Reassembling in a straggling fashion in Templepatrick, the conspirators again failed to agree and Simms abruptly resigned his command. No-one had been found to replace him when they met again on 3 June at the Sheep Ree, a desolate spot on Ballyboley mountain. A vote was taken, and it was decided to postpone an insurrection until the French arrived. When this verdict reached the Antrim village of Ballyeaston, the crowd broke into an uproar and on the spot elected Henry Joy McCracken, a young Belfast cotton-master, to be the overall commander and lead them into action.

McCracken had hours rather than days to draw up his strategy and given the circumstances it was worthy enough for an amateur. He knew that the magistrates were due to meet in Antrim town on 7 June. He sent orders to all the United Irish units in the county to appear in arms that day and overwhelm

The Battle of Ballynahinch, 1798 [detail] by Thomas Robinson. (Office of Public Works)

their local garrisons. He arranged for Randalstown to be attacked, while he and James Hope, with the men of Belfast and South Antrim, would lead the main attack on Antrim town, which was strategically located on the route from Belfast to Ballymena and Derry. A reserve army was to assemble on Donegore Hill, just east of the town. Late on 6 June he issued his famous order: 'Army of Ulster, tomorrow we march on Antrim'.

At first all went like clockwork. The problem was that General Nugent knew more about the plan than any insurgent under McCracken's command, thanks to Nicholas Mageean, a young Catholic farmer from County Down who was a member of the provincial committee. Mageean had been providing information to the authorities for some time, and on Wednesday 6 June he sent an urgent warning of the imminent revolt. At daylight Nugent alerted Major Seddon, who commanded the small garrison in Antrim, and promised to send him reinforcements. Taking a carefully calculated risk, he dispatched a mixed column of regulars, militia and yeomanry from Belfast, and another from General Goldie's command at Lisburn, in the hope of scotching the rebellion on the first day without endangering Belfast.

Meanwhile what the country people would long remember as 'the turnout' was happening all over the east of the county. In the port of Larne the United Irishmen had already attacked the garrison and loyalists during the night, and thousands were in arms on the peninsula of Islandmagee and in the area about Ballycarry, moving westward towards Donegore. Further north on the coast a host assembled on Bellair Hill near Glenarm, commanded by the Presbyterian minister, the Revd Robert Acheson, in a green jacket faced with yellow, white breeches, black hose and silver-buckled shoes. In the centre of the county disciplined bodies of armed men surged into Ballymena, where they would be joined next day by the men of North Antrim, led by young Richard Caldwell. The cradle of the rebellion, however, was the broad fertile valley of the Sixmilewater, where every village that morning produced its quota of men, singing and cheering as they marched to swell the vast concourse on Donegore Hill. Among them was James Orr, the rustic 'bard of Ballycarry' who vividly described the scene as they awaited Nugent's redcoats, bright in arms What impressed him most was the noise:

> The red-wud, warping, wild uproar
>
> Was like a bee scap castin
>
> [like a bee-hive overturned]

Henry Munro, 'chief of the Irish rebels', by Thomas Rowlandson.

Orr's dialect poem is touched with sardonic humour. Many of the rebels were like himself reluctant foot-soldiers, still declaiming the lofty ideals of the French Revolution, but in truth rather frightened and confused about their leaders' aims. No longer, as in the heyday of the Volunteers, were they officered by the gentry and their social superiors. Through the reading societies and the *Northern Star* newspaper they had discovered Tom Paine and educated themselves on the 'rights of man'. While the merchant class were tempted by the economic advantages of union with Britain, rather than separation, the artisans, mechanics and rural labourers were beginning to think more like trade-unionists. James Hope was the outstanding example, a socialist ahead of his time.

Despite his overwhelming superiority in numbers, McCracken waited far too long before entering Antrim through the Scotch Quarter and the tiny garrison had plenty of time to prepare for a heroic defence. Meanwhile the two army columns had a rendezvous two or three miles to the south. Eager for action, Colonel William Lumley, the Etonian who commanded the 22nd Dragoons, obtained permission to move swiftly ahead, and entering the town by the Massereene Bridge, he made the now familiar mistake of launching a cavalry charge at the long pikes. The dragoons took heavy casualties, Lumley was severely wounded, and his cavalrymen were raked with musket fire by Hope's sharpshooters as they retreated. However, it is probably true that Lumley's costly action prevented the insurgents from occupying the whole town, and put them on the defensive. Confusion now began to overtake the insurgent columns arriving from the north and west. The fifth Volunteer cannon, exhumed from under the pews of Templepatrick Presbyterian church, proved a singular disappointment.

When Colonel Durham arrived with the main force he bombarded the town for half an hour, before advancing in to it with the Monaghan Militia, who slew all they met, rebel and welcoming loyalist alike. In two or three hours the battle was over, and McCracken's army had been repulsed on the first day. As the news of Antrim was received there, the huge assembly on Donegore Hill melted away. The rebellion was not over, of course. Ballymena, to the north of Antrim, was occupied by contingents of United Irishmen from the surrounding areas, and became a republic for three days, while its Committee of Public Safety tried desperately to reconstruct a rebel high command. In such towns, however, there was by now a distinct mood of damage limitation among the leading citizens who still had influence over the armed multitudes. When Colonel Clavering, acting without authorisation, offered an amnesty, it was accepted with alacrity, and the roads leading out of Ballymena were piled high with the discarded arms. At Glenarm Acheson had already saved his life by surrendering on terms.

Nugent had been lucky. Belfast was quiet and likely now to remain so. In County Down confusion had reigned in the United Irish leadership after the arrest of Steel Dickson on 5 June, but some of the younger officers, including several probationers for the Presbyterian ministry, took the initiative. David Bailie Warden, who was later to have a distinguished career as a scholar and diplomat in the United States, made an unsuccessful attempt on Newtownards, and then went on to rouse north Down and the Ards peninsula. On Saturday 9 June, Colonel Chetwynd-Stapylton and a detachment of his regiment, the York Fencibles, were ambushed at Saintfield and forced to retreat after losing several of his officers, including his own cousin, Captain William Chetwynd, a circumstance which has misled some chroniclers.

This initial victory (the only one in the Northern rebellion) put great heart into the County Down United Irishmen. After Nugent prudently withdrew all his outposts, most of east Down was at their mercy. A considerable force of the Ards men, equipped with cannon taken from ships in Bangor harbour, marched round the head of Strangford Lough and west towards the centre of

The Hanging of Henry Joy McCracken by John Carey, 1896. (Ulster Museum)

Down, where they joined insurgents from the Saintfield and Ballynahinch area at the Creevy Rocks. Here on Pike Sunday they listened to a sermon preached by the Revd. Thomas Ledlie Birch, and next day they elected Henry Monro, a young Lisburn linen draper, as their commander. Nugent hoped to keep open his line of communication with Dublin through the centre of the county for as long as possible, but the rebels, pushing westward, occupied Ballynahinch and established their main camp at Montalto, the estate of the Earl of Moira.

On the morning of Tuesday 12 June, reassured by the favourable reports from Antrim, Nugent judged it safe to take the field against them with a large force accompanied by half a dozen six-pounders, two howitzers and ammunition wagons. The day was very hot and the progress of the column was slow, though soon to be traced by the smoke of burning farmsteads. Nugent found Saintfield completely deserted and pressed on to Ballynahinch, where he dislodged a rebel outpost on Windmill Hill, and established his headquarters there. He had ordered the Argyll Fencibles stationed at Downpatrick under Colonel George Stewart, to join him and cut off the probable line of rebel retreat. As darkness fell his artillery began the bombardment of Montalto and Ednavady Hill.

What happened there during the night is still unclear and a matter of debate among historians. Large numbers of the insurgents slipped away under the cover of darkness, many demoralised by the cannonade, but there was also a disagreement about tactics. The tired and hungry Monaghan Militia had looted the town and become very drunk. Some of Monro's officers argued for a night attack while the troops were in this state, but were over-ruled by Monro, who decided on an attack at dawn. This was carried out with great courage and determination. The Monaghans were driven back through the streets, their adjutant was killed, and several of their field-guns were taken, but as so often happened in 1798, the insurgents were confused by their own lack of military expertise. Mistaking the bugle calls of the retreating infantry for a signal of the arrival of reinforcements, they faltered, and the British officers, realising what was happening, swiftly ordered the counter-attack.

Soon the United Irishmen were streaming away from Ballynahinch in all directions, only to be cut down by the pursuing cavalry. No quarter was given, and among those who perished in this way was Betsy Gray, a young girl who had accompanied her brother and fiancé to the rebel camp. In time she became a figure of legend, an Ulster Joan of Arc, who was depicted as riding into battle on a white horse and holding aloft a green banner.

The battle of Ballynahinch was the most serious encounter of the northern rising, but it was not on the scale of the battles of New Ross or Vinegar Hill in County Wexford. The battles of Antrim and Ballynahinch were followed by harsh retribution. McCracken and Monro were captured and hanged, along with scores of less prominent rebels. It was to a large extent a Presbyterian rebellion, and it marked the end of the Dissenters' sense of political exclusion which had strengthened their alliance with Catholics elsewhere in Ireland. Some twenty Presbyterian ministers and probationers were involved, and two were executed. Though the principles of the original United Irishmen had inculcated a brotherhood of affection among Irishmen, the effect of 1798 in the North was painfully to emphasise divisions which already existed in religion and society. Catholic soldiers fought with Protestant rebels, and sometimes with Orange yeomanry. Neighbour hunted down neighbour, Church of Ireland was set against Presbyterian, landlord against tenant, engendering feuds among families which have lasted almost to the present. Apart from an assembly of several thousand United Irishmen near Maghera, County Derry, which quickly dispersed, the rebellion was confined to the counties of Antrim and Down, the area east of the Bann. Astonishingly, not one of the other seven Ulster counties took part. Republicanism, which was intended to free the Irish people from sectarianism, became in the nineteenth century part of the dispute.

Chapter Twelve

'Keeping up the flame': (General) Joseph Holt

Ruan O'Donnell

In August 1898, when the centenary celebrations of the Rebellion of 1798 approached their climax, George McSweeney wrote: 'of all the leaders of the United Irishmen perhaps there was no career more remarkable than Joseph Holt, and yet there is no actor in the great drama of '98 to whom it is harder to assign a just place in the history of the period'. McSweeney pinpointed the *Memoirs of Joseph Holt* (1838) as the principal source of the ambiguity surrounding its ostensible author as they presented him as a man who had been 'forced into rebellion' and 'cared nothing for reform'. It was not then realised that this false impression was largely the responsibility of the editor, Thomas Crofton Croker, chief clerk of the Admiralty and a noted folklorist, who interpolated many digressions depicting Holt as a condescending anti-Catholic bigot.

Holt's thoroughly unpleasant literary persona, when added to the somewhat suspicious fact that he survived 1798 and returned from exile in Australia, did not endear him to those in the thrall of the influential historian Fr. P.F. Kavanagh. The *Memoirs*, paradoxically, were also vilified by elements of the unionist readership Croker's revisions had been intended to mollify. Isaac Butt's review for the *Dublin University Magazine* claimed that the two volumes were 'a disgusting farrago of blood boultered egotism, the irreligious pulings of affected religion, and the conscientious sensibilities of a wholesale murderer'.

Holt's status also suffered because of disinterest in the Wicklow theatre and the elevation of Michael Dwyer as the county's alternate hero figure by the 1870s. Dwyer was an eminently suitable substitute having spent five years on the run in the mountains during which time he had many dramatic escapes and conspired with Robert Emmet. By the 140th anniversary of the Rebellion in 1938 plans to honour Holt on the site of his Roundwood farm stalled as soon as the foundation stone was laid and Cork historian Sean Ó Coindelbháin suggested a few years later that the Wicklowman's name be erased from that city's 1798 memorial in view of his alleged treachery.

Contrary to the popular record, Holt was arguably the most militant leader of the Rebellion. He was also one of the highest ranking Church of Ireland commanders produced by the Leinster theatre and ultimately wielded greater authority than that enjoyed by his impressive co-religionists Anthony Perry of Inch and William Barker of Enniscorthy. This circumstance is only partly attributable to the flourishing of a pluralist organisation in a county where over one-fifth of the population were non-Catholic. Of real consequence were the circumstances of Holt's command, which, in the aftermath of the mass surrenders of July 1798, was the largest body of its kind under arms. It was, furthermore, the only faction poised to intensify the struggle when the French landed in Mayo in August 1798 at which time 'General Holt' was indisputably the best known and most feared rebel leader.

Holt served a brief stint as a recruiter for the 32nd regiment and as a Volunteer in Arklow but it was his experiences as a baronial sub-constable in the late 1780s that developed the nascent skills of a guerrilla fighter. He was reputedly an exceptionally effective and fearless manhunter in Wicklow, Wexford, Dublin and Kildare: a well-informed correspondent of the *Edinburgh Advertiser* claimed that Holt's prowess in the role of 'thief-taker general...inspire[d] terror in breasts before not susceptible to fear'. Possessed of a 'stern and manly aspect, strong, and well made, singularly athletic, about five feet eleven inches high', Holt was credited in October 1798 with 'those talents best calculated to impose on the desperate multitude with whom he acts'.

Work as a cloth assessor in Rathdrum obliged Holt to visit the remote mountain communities where he enhanced an already comprehensive and reputedly unrivalled knowledge of county geography. This familiarity was exploited by him during or shortly after the spring of 1797 when he and at least three of his four brothers joined the United Irishmen. Joseph became a recruiter and was evidently elected to the position of captain before the close of 1797. Holt forged links with republicans from Dublin's south city who fostered the conspiracy in south Leinster and assumed national control when the provincial directory was decimated by arrests in March 1798. He was personally acquainted with key organisers such as William Putnam McCabe of Belfast and Fr. John Martin of Drogheda prior to the Rebellion and clearly liaised with them on behalf of the north Wicklow sector.

This profile and the work of informers ensured that Holt was a marked man several weeks prior to the outbreak of Rebellion. Wicklow was gripped from early April by the full force of state terror and Holt was on the run in the mountains before 10 May 1798 when his Mullinaveigue farmhouse was burned. This attack punished an overture by him to two Antrim militiamen billeted on the property and local commander Major Joseph Hardy claimed that it was the

The status of Joseph Holt suffered as a result of the elevation of Michael Dwyer as Wicklow's hero.

first reprisal of its kind to receive his sanction. Holt's autobiography, even in its original form, however, is not an entirely reliable account of his experiences in this period as it was geared towards generating income and respectability in early nineteenth-century Ireland. Much of what he obscured can be traced from Castle intelligence papers and the testimony of those who fought with him as collected by Luke Cullen in the early to mid-1800s.

Elements of Wicklow's 14,000 United Irishmen were amongst the first engaged on the night of 23 May 1798 and by dawn hundreds had mobilised in the western barony of Talbotstown. Baltinglass, Stratford-on-Slaney and Dunlavin were attacked on the 24th but little of consequence happened in Holt's native Ballinacor barony until five days later when he led 300 men from the Devil's Glen to Annamoe to burn the home of ultra-loyalist magistrate Thomas Hugo. They were temporarily dispersed by a military relief force who unwittingly broke up one of three rebel columns preparing to attack the garrison of Newtownmountkennedy on the 30th. Holt's men were consequently absent when over 1,000 of their comrades were repulsed from the strategic town, a check which was compounded the following day by the loss of Blackmore Hill camp near Blessington.

With an early city attack postponed and large scale mobilisation in north Wicklow inhibited by early defeats and widespread army atrocities, Holt was one of several leaders who went south to Wexford where matters were known to have taken a more favourable course from 27 May. Supplies were issued to the company under the command of 'Colonel Holt of Wicklow' at Corbet Hill and/or Carrickbyrne camp prior to the attack on New Ross on 5 June but they were evidently part of the massive army that was not committed to the battle. Another Wicklow group under William Byrne of Ballymanus returned to Mount Pleasant camp near Tinahely where around 2,000 quickly rallied as the 'Ballymanus division' which operated with the north Wexford army. Holt's faction retraced their steps to north Wicklow where they awaited news of the anticipated breakthrough at Arklow.

Fighting in the Wicklow mountains was an attractive option for the native rebels who could traverse the ranges extending from the Rathfarnham district of south county Dublin as far as Wexford with little fear of interference. The near Roadless, poorly mapped and boggy terrain of central Wicklow was so difficult of access that the army's potentially devastating asset of cavalry was almost useless beyond the role of reconnaissance and their cannons nothing but an exhausting encumbrance. Battle against light infantry could easily be avoided by the rebels, moreover, once the rudimentary precaution of posting sentries was taken as red coats were easily spotted on a bleak and virtually treeless highland landscape. Excellent weather in the summer of 1798 minimised the hazards of exposure while subsistence was provided by the huge quantities of livestock abandoned by the fearful loyalists and neutrals who had evacuated Carnew, Tinahely, Shillelagh, Donoughmore and Ashford. With no supply lines to forfeit and none of the heavy baggage that slowed their adversaries, rebel mobility in the Wicklow mountains posed a threat to which the government had no solution.

Michael Dwyer.

Defeat at Arklow on 9 June put paid to attempts to break out of Wexford by which time Holt commanded in excess of 1,000 Ballinacor, Rathdown and Newcastle rebels and exerted influence over allied corps from Kildare and Dublin. Frustration at the Arklow reverse was vented by the burning of over twenty loyalist homes in the Roundwood area on the night of 14 June which were singled out from the general citizenry with great discipline and discrimination. Skirmishes with the Rathdrum yeoman cavalry and Reay Highlanders ensued for several days in which both sides enjoyed minor victories of little strategic consequence.

The government victory at Vinegar Hill on 21 June precipitated the juncture of all Wicklow forces three days later in the hills overlooking the Carlow border town of Hacketstown. Garret Byrne of Ballymanus and Edward Fitzgerald of Newpark had led their north Wexford/south Wicklow column from Enniscorthy through 'Needham's gap' to the Wicklow mountains where they drew Holt's men as well as new recruits to their banner. Holt's precise role during the battle on the 25th is unclear but it was claimed that his horse was shot from under him during the day long assault. No stratagem of the cannon-less rebels succeeded in rooting the defenders out of their stone barracks but consolation was taken the following day when the abandoned building was fired by a rebel patrol. A less concerted effort to storm Carnew also failed on 30 June for identical reasons, although the day had already yielded a famous victory at nearby Ballyellis where a masterful ambush had been laid by Holt. Ballyellis consolidated his growing stature within the officer committee that controlled the rump forces and he demonstrated a degree of tactical genius in organising the deployment of insurgents who inflicted forty-nine fatalities on their Ancient Britons, 5th Dragoon Guards and yeomen enemies.

A disappointing skirmish at Ballyrahan Hill near Tinahely on 2 July killed two yeomanry captains and seventeen of their men but impressed many rebels with a sense of futility. Once again loyalist possession of a fortified redoubt had thwarted rebel intentions. Unwilling to campaign in Wexford where supplies were increasingly difficult to obtain and military opposition stronger than ever, Holt detached his followers from the Ballymanus division and withdrew to the relative security of north Wicklow. This transpired to be a prescient decision as the inauspicious conditions of the Wexford theatre frustrated the plans of their comrades. The trend to accept the proffered amnesty terms greatly accelerated there in the first week of July when the vast majority of insurgents retired from the rebellion. Several thousand of those determined to press on were obliged to follow Fitzgerald and Garret Byrne back into Wicklow where they combined forces with Holt at Whelp Rock on the slopes of Blackmore Hill.

A presence in the Wicklow mountains yielded little scope for the rebels to prosecute the Rebellion to a satisfactory conclusion and it was agreed to trek

into Meath to gather recruits en route to south Ulster. Holt's deep-rooted opposition to the plan and his conviction that they should instead attack Newtownmountkennedy did not deter him from accompanying the main force from Whelp Rock into Meath where they met with disaster after disaster. A costly repulse at Clonard on 11 July and a government assault on their camp at Ryndville Hill the following day fractured the fatigued rebels who had already shed more deserters than gained recruits. Holt's status in the army increased when he arranged a rear guard action which slowed the dragoons and probably prevented the total rout of the insurgents when vulnerable in retreat. He was twice wounded in this endeavour and was cut off from the main body when they were again brought to battle and defeated at Knightstown bog on the 14th. This loss resulted in the near complete dissipation of the United Irish struggle beyond the Wicklow mountains.

Following the midlands debacle Holt was the only leader of note both willing to persevere and capable of commanding a sizeable body of men. Almost all his surviving associates surrendered under terms that admitted them to the pact negotiated by the high-ranking 'state prisoners' who had been arrested before the Rebellion. Holt had no intention of compromising and prior to November 1798 made Glenmalure, Whelp Rock and the King's River valley the principal resorts of up to 2,000 rebels. Government concern at the prospect of a 'brigand war' smouldering in Wicklow and possibly emanating from the county caused them to dispatch General John Moore to implement a proactive amnesty program. Moore and the Marquis of Huntley established a camp in Imaal in the last days of July where 1,200 rebels were pardoned. Holt's ranks were reduced to a 'mere band' by this moderate approach but mushroomed again when disgruntled loyalists took it upon themselves to persecute retiring insurgents.

Holt became a figure of national interest from late July 1798 when his militancy, charisma and the attrition of his peers ensured that he enjoyed a position of uncomplicated leadership. His orders were not mediated through officer committees or subject to the amateurish whims of a theoretical commander-in-chief. Democratic forums, however dear to the ideologically motivated United Irishmen, had no place in warfare, and had engendered bad strategy and indecision in the most decisive of all human pursuits. The peculiar dangers of operating in the mountains may have encouraged junior leaders to either accept Holt's decisions or to pursue their own agenda in their home areas. In this theatre his maturity, proven ability and physically imposing presence elicited respect.

While the Imaal men attached to Michael Dwyer came and went from the main force as they pleased and were often reluctant to venture outside west Wicklow, units from Glenmalure, Redcross, Arklow, Seven Churches, Aughrim and the Bray area generally accepted Holt's orders until October 1798 when matters became strained. Although far from absolute, Holt's authority enabled him to implement militarily sound practices that had not been possible earlier in the rebellion. An important feature was that the rebels underwent regular training exercises in Glenmalure which improved their responsiveness to orders. This was beneficial to their deployment in combat which was particularly difficult in the exposed Wicklow mountains where friend and foe could generally see

The Battle of New Ross – prior to the attack supplies were issued to a 'Colonel Holt of Wicklow'.
(National Library of Ireland)

each other for miles beyond firing range. Speed was the factor upon which the success of the rebels was predicated and their lives dependent.

Holt subdivided his followers into gun and pike units who rehearsed ambush techniques and closing with their opponents. The fruits of these preparations were seen in late July 1798 when the unexpected arrival of the 60th, 89th and 100th regiments in Glenmalure was met with a disciplined retreat under fire into Imaal. They also experimented with tactics and repulsed 300 Fermanagh militiamen at Knockalt on 1 October by a devastating combination of feints, concealed entrenchments and concentrated firepower. Ten soldiers were left for dead as the survivors fled without their weapons and kit. Insurgent confidence in Holt's abilities, moreover, was demonstrated by their quick recovery from the shock of a night attack being sprung on them at Greenan bridge around 10 September. Their initial panic subsided when Holt shouted orders for a counterattack, in Miles Byrne's words, 'with the voice of a stentor'.

A positive by-product of the amnesty program was that it stripped Holt of his less resolute and unfit men who were replaced by around 150 defectors from the Antrim, Leitrim, Sligo, King's County and other militia regiments. These were amongst the most highly motivated and effective insurgents due to their training, equipment and the harshness with which their apostasy was treated by government. The rebels in Wicklow were far from malcontented fanatics or bandits and apparently waged war in the hope of spearheading a renewed insurrection with French aid. On hearing of Humbert's landing Holt undertook a major recruiting drive in the Blackwater district of Wexford, west Carlow, Kildare and Dublin. Blessington was occupied within hours of its evacuation by General Moore's western-bound troops and while it proved impossible to attempt the mooted city attack, Wicklow was convulsed by the heaviest fighting in two months. In the last week of August and the first of September fatal clashes occurred near Coolgreany, Clone Hill, Mucklagh Hill, Blessington, Greenan, Keadeen and Glenmalure. This upsurge continued even after the arrival of news of Humbert's final defeat at Ballinamuck on 8 September.

Holt's fortunes culminated on 19 September when at very short notice he led around 500 rebels across almost twenty kilometres of highland to capture Aughrim. Having engaged and then pursued the Rathdrum cavalry and Hunter Gowan's 'Black Mob' garrison out of range the insurgents set about vandalising local yeomanry homes. This raid lent credence to alarmist reports which asserted that the rebels had menaced Bray, Dundrum, Rathfarnham and even villages as far afield as Celbridge in Kildare. Holt evinced an awareness of the psychological aspect of warfare and issued several threatening letters such as one which warned Arklow's garrison in late August that he 'would speedily be among them and would not spare a single orangeman'. Loyalist clamour obliged Lord Cornwallis to dispatch 2,000 extra troops to the county in late September on yet another fruitless mission to eradicate the rebels.

The comparatively disciplined and purposeful actions of Holt's force made an deep impression on the Leinster gentry who realised that their activities constituted a major source of instability in the province. Lady Sarah Napier noted the disappointment of her tenantry on hearing of the French defeat but realised that they 'put a good face on it, still hankering after a chance of a new force, which is collecting in Wicklow, under a clever man called Holt, who *rejects* mob, and *chooses* his associates. This keeps up the flame'. The London based *Courier* carried over sixty-five reports concerning Holt between 5 September and 28 November 1798 and coverage of his exploits in the French *Bien Informe* apparently made him 'the symbol of Irish resistance'.

Resistance was characterised if not sustained by a ruthless program of assassination and arson against Wicklow loyalists who incurred the second highest losses of any county in 1798. Dozens of informers, active loyalists and Orangemen were put to death by Holt's men to safeguard themselves and their families. Many were members of the atrocity-prone yeomanries of Carnew, Tinahely and Rathdrum for whom no friendly intercession was likely;

Hessians and Ancient Britons were typically executed to avenge their brutality towards prisoners, women and non-combatants. The context for such violence was the cold-blooded killings of at least 106 jailed rebels in Dunlavin, Carnew, Ballymore-Eustace and Newtownmountkennedy between 23 May and 1 June 1798. Resentment at pre-rebellion excesses was sharpened by more recent events which included the massacre of twenty-seven civilians at Aughrim on 22 June 1798. Tensions were further heightened by the army's extensive scorched earth policy which paralleled the routine destruction by the rebels of all slate-roofed buildings and stone-built premises that were located in the vicinity of their mountain resorts.

The seemingly interminable depredations in Wicklow troubled the Cornwallis administration who sought to restore tranquillity in advance of the Act of Union. When the 'infamously celebrated' Holt proved responsive to offers of a negotiated surrender no effort was spared to effect his capitulation on terms short of self-exile or 'state prisoner' status. His arrival at Powerscourt on 10 November 1798 was brokered by the La Touches of Delgany and other north Wicklow families who guaranteed that his life would be spared if he came in. Castle spies reported that Holt first conferred with city leaders and had dismissed his remaining subordinates on learning that French naval losses made their efforts untenable if not unjustifiable. Opposed to frittering away his men in a militarily pointless and gruelling winter campaign, and with £300 on his head, Holt agreed to go become a 'voluntary exile for life' in New South Wales. This brought to an end co-ordinated armed resistance by the United Irishmen in 1798.

In 1804 Philip Gidley King, governor of the struggling penal settlements of New South Wales, had cause to berate Holt's 'inflammant character' which he claimed had contributed much towards the severe unrest in colony. The Wicklowman had been sent out as a free man on the *Minerva* in August 1799 and was shortly afterwards punished for complicity in the United Irish plots of 1800. Many former comrades had looked once more to Holt for revolutionary leadership and he featured prominently in the planning stages of the violent Castle Hill revolt of March 1804. This was Holt's last foray into republican sedition and he afterwards settled down to a life of some prosperity until his pardon enabled him to return to Ireland in 1813. Holt died in Dún Laoghaire in May 1826 and was buried in a family plot in Carrickbrennan cemetery, Monkstown. This grave, far from being a more convenient Bodenstown, was overgrown and forgotten until restored by a school's project in the 1980s. Fittingly, Holt's Irish, American and Australian relatives jointly unveiled a new memorial to their remarkable ancestor in Mullinaveigue on 10 May 1998.

Chapter Thirteen

'Educated Whiteboyism': The Cork tithe war, 1798–99

James G. Patterson

In the wake of the 1798 rebellion a wave of agrarian agitation swept Munster. Superficially the disaffection—centred on the counties of Limerick, Cork and Tipperary, although there were incidents throughout the province— seemed to be the latest manifestation of the long-term phenomenon of 'Whiteboyism'. This generic term denotes the activities of the agrarian secret societies that first appeared in the south of Ireland in the early 1760s. The Whiteboys are most commonly depicted as reactive, with a primary focus on the redress of local grievance, and, in reality, the post-'98 movement in County Cork continued to address the traditional concerns of tithes and rents. Yet it is evident that a fundamental transformation had occurred by the winter of 1798–99. Prior to the 1790s the agrarian secret societies exhibited an extreme reluctance to utilise capital force. As Thomas Bartlett noted, 'these essentially conservative protests were not, by eighteenth-century standards, particularly violent … there was much intimidation and threatening behaviour, but significantly death was rarely inflicted by the protesters'. But in the aftermath of 1798 agrarian activists in County Cork demonstrated a remarkable willingness to employ extreme levels of physical violence. Perhaps more importantly, for a period of years following 1798 the secret societies supported the overthrow of the socio-political system via the medium of a French invasion, a decidedly proactive motivation.

Post-rebellion disaffection was evident in County Cork as early as September 1798, when the authorities arrested two blacksmiths caught manufacturing pikes near Oysterhaven. A short time later, unknown individuals cut down 30 ash trees for use as pike handles. On 14 September a relatively minor incident occurred that foreshadowed the strikingly brutal events that were to become commonplace in the months that followed. That night intruders cut off, or 'cropt', the ears of six horses belonging to a man who resided on the northern outskirts of Cork city. The motivation ascribed to the crime was the fact that the individual in question had 'taken his tithes'. In other words, the animals' owner was a 'tithe-farmer', one of the despised middlemen capitalists who purchased the right to collect tithes for Protestant clergymen in response to the opportunities offered by the emerging market economy during the second half of the eighteenth century. These men of business were inevitably more efficient and ruthless than the clergy in extracting maximum rates and as a result were often bitterly resented. It is hardly surprising that tithe-farmers had been one of the primary targets of the earlier Whiteboy and Rightboy redresser movements in Cork.

In fact, what can most accurately be described as an overt tithe war raged in County Cork throughout the winter of 1798–99. This simple reality was obvious by January 1799, when members of the Cork establishment described the impact the anti-tithe agitation was having locally. That month, a Mr Longford reported from Cork city that 'In the eastern part of this county … not a tithe farmer or proctor dare show his head'. Similarly from north Cork a Mr Freeman wrote that 'Notices threatening death to all dealers in tithes, should they proceed to decree any person, have been universally posted … at every chapel from Churchtown to Millstreet'. Most significantly, the anti-tithe agitation was coordinated, as 'emissaries' were known to be criss-crossing the county holding 'nightly' meetings. Indeed, by February the situation had degenerated to the point where it drew the attention of Lord Lieutenant Cornwallis, who bluntly informed the duke of Portland that 'In County Cork the usual resistance to the payment of tithes continues accompanied by the cruel persecution of those employed in collecting them'.

Specific outrages included the murder 'in a most barbarous and savage manner' of a tithe-farmer and his assistant at a house only six miles from Cork city on the night of Saturday 19 January. The victim, a farmer named Timothy McCarthy, paid the ultimate penalty for having rented the tithes of the parish of Carrigrohanebeg. Similarly, at Glanworth in north Cork a band of so-called 'rebels' met nightly in 'great force'. This group contained a sizeable mounted element, which permitted them to operate over a large area. Members of the band attempted to murder a Mr Hanlon at Castletownroche and, although the primary target escaped, his under-bailiff was beaten 'almost to death'. A particularly brutal attack took place in Rathcormac, where a number of men forced their way into the home of Revd Mr Blackwood, an Anglican cleric. In addition to destroying Blackwood's tithe records, the likely objective of their visit, the intruders also butchered his processor, a member of the Elgin Fencibles, who had the misfortune to be in the house at the time. After killing the soldier, they 'cut the body in small pieces'. In like fashion, although with less sanguinary results, marauders entered the residence of Revd Campion

'Martial law in '98', from a painting by Henry Allan, (National Library of Ireland)

and destroyed tithe notes valued at £200; they also grievously injured two of the minister's servants. Near the end of January another process-server was decapitated near Kildorrery, while several others were severely beaten. Indeed, the level of violence evident in the anti-tithe campaign of the winter of 1798–99 compares quite unfavourably to that of its most recent antecedent, the widespread 'Rightboy' movement of the 1780s. The Rightboys, who similarly focused much of their attention on the issue of tithes, were responsible for as few as four deaths during the six years in which they were active in County Cork between 1785 and 1791.

What, then, explains the willingness of post-'98 agrarian movements in south Munster to utilise extreme physical violence? The most plausible explanation is the brutalisation of Irish society in the 1790s. The ideologically driven war with revolutionary France and the rise of radical republicanism in Ireland engendered tremendous fear in Irish loyalists and the government, who responded with increasingly savage repression. The litany of atrocity between 1793 and 1798 is well known. The military shot down some 250 people during the militia riots of 1793; hundreds, if not thousands, of Defenders were killed or sent to the fleet between 1794 and 1798; the Orange Order drove between 5000 and 7000 Catholics from their homes in Armagh during 1795-96; the bloodbath of the Rebellion of 1798 resulted in somewhere between 20,000 and 30,000 deaths in a few short months. Simply put, the state tacitly sanctioned the creation of an environment in which capital force was the norm.

In addition to the three dozen executions that took place in Cork in 1798, the neighbouring counties of Limerick and Tipperary offered the people of Cork proximate examples of loyalist and government-sponsored terror. Over a three-week period in June 1798, 76 men were tried by courts martial at Limerick on charges related to the rebellion. Seven of these individuals were executed and 22 others transported. In Tipperary the rabid high sheriff, Thomas Judkin Fitzgerald, waged a vicious flogging campaign prior to the rebellion against United Irishmen, both real and imagined. Moreover, officially sanctioned terror in the form of courts martial persisted into mid-1800 (i.e. two years after the rebellion). For example, a massive wave of agrarian agitation in the west was brutally suppressed during the winter and spring of 1798-99. At Galway over 73 cases were heard, resulting in eighteen capital convictions and a like number of transportations. Similar trials were held at Ballinrobe and Castlebar in Mayo, leading to at least 22 death sentences. In 1800, as a result of Defender activity, a major court martial was convened at Ballymena, Co. Antrim, where seventeen capital convictions were ultimately carried into effect. Indeed, as late as December 1803 in counties Tipperary and Waterford (areas largely untouched by the political turmoil of the 1790s) special commissions sentenced seventeen men to hang. In reference to these latter cases, Thomas Prendergast observed: 'His inquiries into the causes and effects of the outrages [that had led to the trials] had nothing of a political tendency'. Instead, 'their objects were to drive from the neighbourhood strange workmen... or to interfere with the letting of farms'. Prendergast concluded: 'The present disturbances, frightful as they are, are nothing more than a revival of the old Whiteboy spirit that [for] fifty years past has at different and frequent periods prevailed'. Yet a fundamental transformation had occurred: only about 50 deaths, including government-sanctioned executions, can be attributed to the combined disturbances of the Whiteboys, Rightboys, Oakboys and Steelboys between 1760 and 1790.

Another striking divergence in post-'98 agrarianism in County Cork is revealed in a manifesto posted at Glanworth in January 1799. The motivational forces that drove the earlier secret societies were aptly summarised by Jim Smyth as follows: 'None of these movements challenged the system of land ownership, or sought to abolish rents or tithes. Rather they agitated for a reduction of those exactions to levels sanctioned by custom as fair'. In contrast,

'This is the Head of a Traitor' by James Henry Brocas. (National Library of Ireland)

the Glanworth manifesto demanded the outright abolition of tithes rather than their mitigation. It further forbade 'any man to pay or take' tithes. Nor was this document an isolated aberration, for evidence revealed at the courts martial assembled to deal with the agrarian crisis in March 1799 established that '[the] people ... by their oath are bound to pay no taxes or tithes, and to assemble when called'.

The significance of this transformation should not be underestimated. By endeavouring to eliminate tithes in their entirety, the post-'98 secret societies called into question the legitimacy of a central facet of the Protestant Ascendancy, the right of the established church to levy taxes on the Catholic majority. Thus an extremely important evolution is revealed. The Whiteboys during the 1760s never questioned the entitlement of the established church to collect tithes. However, mercenary middlemen tithe-farmers, who charged rates above the customary, if not technically legal, level, were targeted as violators of the moral economy. Similarly, the Rightboys did not directly challenge the Protestant minister's ownership and collection rights, although in addition to tithe-farmers the Rightboys also often attacked proctors, who for a price did the collecting for the actual owners. Yet during the formative decade of the 1790s efforts to limit tithes to customary levels were supplanted by endeavours to eliminate them in their entirety. Thus the very legitimacy of the established church was called into question.

The motivating force behind this transformation was the Society of United Irishmen, which had made its most dramatic inroads in the highly commercialised tillage districts of east Cork during 1797. It is hardly coincidental that these same parishes were the ones most affected by the anti-tithe agitation of 1798–99. Along with participatory democracy, the United Irishmen promised to abolish the taxes and tithes. By injecting the Enlightenment and Thomas Paine into the picture, the United Irishmen pointed to the irrationality and simple unfairness of a system whereby the often desperately poor majority supported the church of a far-better-off minority.

The evidence of this process is substantial. In a meeting at Cloyne in October 1797 the Cork United Irish leader, John Sweeny, addressed an assembled body. He knew his audience well for he focused his speech on the issue of tithes. Most importantly, as Kevin Whelan explained, Sweeny pointed to the need to eliminate the 'state-sponsored church', exhorting the people 'not to pay [tithes] ... and to do all in our power to obstruct the said tithe being paid'. The tithe war of 1798–99 is proof positive that the lesson was taken to heart. Thus, at least for a time, the radical republicanism of the United Irishmen intersected with the redress of agrarian grievance. The end result was a highly focused hybrid, the 'educated Whiteboy'.

Perhaps of even greater importance, the success of the anti-tithe agitation—and it was highly successful indeed, at least in the short term—strongly suggests that large numbers of people expected to avoid the penalties traditionally associated with non-payment. In turn, the only plausible explanation for this assumption is a widespread popular belief that a French invasion would soon overturn the Protestant ascendancy and disestablish the church that sustained it.

Evidence for the broad-based anticipation of foreign assistance is substantial. A Mr Kirby, who lived at Tallow on the western extremity of County Waterford, expressed 'great concern' over the 'unpleasant state of the country' in a letter to Lord Castlereagh written in mid-January 1799. Although his home district was 'tolerably quiet', the neighbouring east Cork barony of Kinnatalloon was 'in a dreadful state of disturbance' as 'scarcely a night [passed] without a robbery attended with savage cruelty'. Kirby identified the responsible parties as a 'well-armed' band operating from the village of Conna, headed by a deserter from the Clare Militia named Michael Bryan. Most ominously, Kirby warned: 'They look forward with confidential hope to the arrival of a French force on the southern coast ... [and] when that ... occurs they will rise in a mass'. Similarly, a Mr Harding believed that the 'repeated acts of outrage' were a means of 'preparing the minds of the lower orders' for participation in a rising planned in conjunction with a French landing. In the Blarney area the people talked 'openly of rising', while the disaffected felled trees within two miles of the Liberties of Cork city for use as pike handles. Furthermore, a county committee was believed to hold meetings in the house of a farmer named Buckley at Whitechurch, where a provincial committee had met 'often' during the preceding winter.

Of greatest concern to local loyalists were the persistent rumours of an imminent rising, although all sources of intelligence acknowledged that this would not take place in the absence of a French invasion. In fact, for several years following 1799 the ebb and flow of agrarian agitation in Cork closely mirrored the degree of anticipation of invasion, and it was not until the French defeat at Trafalgar in 1805 that this connection was permanently severed.

Throughout the winter of 1798–99 agrarian depredations continued to plague the propertied in County Cork. Near Blarney in early March 'rebels' burned three houses, two at Grenagh and one belonging to a tithe proctor at Knockilly. On the night of 18 March a man named Creedon, who lived in the Liberties of Cork city, had six cattle destroyed as punishment for having rented land out from under a family named Connell. The approach of spring was accompanied by increasingly shrill cries from local loyalists for decisive action by the government; as one gentleman asserted, 'We must outrage the constitution ... by acts of severity [before] we can preserve it'. In response, the military scoured the countryside, taking up the members of three separate agrarian cells, totalling some 36 men. More significantly, the commander of the southern military district, the exceedingly brutal General Gerard Lake, placed the counties of Limerick, Tipperary and Cork under martial law.

As arbitrary military justice rapidly supplanted civil law in County Cork, 'judges determined not to try rebels and the Grand Juries of the city and county … left them to be tried by courts martial'. By 23 March, Lake felt that the imposition of military law was having the desired effect: 'The country is quiet and every report from the different parts of the district gives reason to hope that tranquillity will soon be restored, as the dread which the people have of courts martial will keep them quiet till the French come'. Similarly, General Myers, commanding the garrison at Cork city, confidently informed his superiors on 26 March that he had arrested twenty men for houghing cattle, thereby putting an end to the 'mischief'.

Yet the courts martial also revealed some rather unsettling facts to the authorities. The difficulty the government experienced in obtaining testimony against the accused was demonstrative of widespread popular support for the secret societies. Moreover, General Lake found '[the] people universally sworn throughout the district', confirming the broad-based participatory nature of post-'98 agrarianism in Munster.

Despite the establishment of summary military justice in March, outrages, albeit on a diminished scale, continued to disturb Cork. The most shocking episode was the assassination at Macroom in April of Robert Hutchinson, a prominent member of the local gentry. A party of six assailants graphically demonstrated the degree to which the deferential conventions of the moral economy had collapsed in the county by the winter of 1799, when one of them thrust a pike through Hutchinson's heart on the staircase of his home. Dozens of arrests ensued and on 14 May the authorities executed five 'United Irishmen' for complicity in the murder. Their heads were then displayed as an awful example on Macroom's bridewell.

Cornwallis was sufficiently troubled by this event to order an investigation into the state of affairs of the entire southern military district. The man assigned to this duty, General Clarke, duly travelled through much of the south-west of Ireland during April and May. In his report to the viceroy, Clarke identified the complex nature of the agitation and was also harshly critical of local landlords, comparing them quite unfavourably to their counterparts in England:

> It appears from the evidence given at most of the Courts Martial that the lower order (particularly the murderers of the late Mr Hutchinson) have determined to murder every gentleman in the country evidently with a

view to drive them from their homes and divide their estates, or at least to intimidate them, so that they may rent the land at their own price. The great sources of these diabolical principals seem to spring from the dislike to tithes ... The middle man is likewise a great grievance as from his inordinate rapacity in letting his land to the cottager who is unable to pay his rent and support his family with any kind of comfort owing to the rate of labour which is regulated by the landlord. I am sorry to add that gentlemen do not in general treat their inferiors with the kindness and humanity people of that station of life experience from the higher orders in England.

Yet having allowed for the agrarian focus of the discontent, Clarke summarised that he had 'every reason to believe that the disposition of the people is not good ... they are ready to rise should the French land in this country'.

In the end, some sense of the scale and ultimate success of the anti-tithe campaign of 1798-99 can be gleaned from a 'report on the outrages committed in the diocese of Cloyne'. The author, in all likelihood an ecclesiastical official of the established church, explained the impact of the movement as follows: 'Very few will attempt to serve processes for tithes, the proctors in general have given up their books and arrears for 1798-99 unpaid, while [the] clergy [are] reduced to distress'. In fact, as late as 1802 tithe-holders in County Cork were attempting to recoup the revenues lost in 1798-99. Although parliament passed a compensation act 'for the benefit of clergy whose tithes were withheld in 1798–99', the difficulties involved in their actual collection remained formidable. Indeed, Richard Orpen, high sheriff of County Cork, prudently resisted requests from tithe-owners in the east Muskerry parishes of Inishcarra and Aghabulloge to provide small cavalry detachments as escorts for collectors, arguing that 'in order to put into effectual force the provisions of this act, which is a service highly obnoxious ... it would require in this extensive county no small military force ... to aid civilian power'.

Chapter Fourteen

'An act of power & corruption'?
The Union debate

Patrick M. Geoghegan

The passing of the Act of Union (1800) was one of the most controversial and contested events in modern Irish history. The historiography has reflected this with interpretations divided on key elements of how and why it was achieved, and at what cost. Lacking in the doomed heroism of the 1798 rebellion, or the other requisite ingredients essential for any popular commemoration, its bicentenary went largely unnoticed. Nevertheless the Union remains one of the most divisive and defining moments of modern Irish political history. Even today, the mere mention of the Act evokes strong feelings in Ireland, and it remains a visible and potent symbol of some of the continuing problems on the island. In many ways the history of the past two hundred has been dominated by the measure, and the various responses and reactions to it.

For many the key debate about the Union has always concerned how it was passed. Opponents of the measure at the time were quick to provide their own interpretation, one which was generally accepted by nationalists in the nineteenth century. The allegation was that the Union passed in 'an orgy of corruption'; the argument was that it was an unpopular measure forced through an unwilling parliament, and a hostile country, by the power and money of the British government. This exposition was best developed by Jonah Barrington, in his various memoirs, and Henry Grattan jnr., in his life of his father, and finally culminated in the poem that was soon taught in every school in Ireland:

How did they pass the Union?

By perjury and fraud;

By slaves who sold their land for gold,

As Judas sold his God.

The Great Parliament of Ireland, 1790, by Henry Barraud and John Hayter. (Campbell College, Belfast)

Few disputed the younger Grattan's assertion that the Union had passed illegally, and that it was 'an act of power and corruption'. While judicious historians like W.E.H. Lecky denied the more extravagant claims, such as the allegation that secret service money had been used, there remained a consensus that the Irish parliament had been infected, and fatally undermined, by what Lecky termed 'a virus of corruption'. One of the first full accounts of the measure, *A history of the legislative union of Great Britain and Ireland* (1887) by T.D. Ingram, attempted clumsily to ignore these charges, and was ignored in turn.

The corruption thesis went largely unchallenged in the twentieth century until 1966 when G.C. Bolton published his classic study *The passing of the Irish Act of Union*. Bolton contested the existing orthodoxy by returning to first principles, and examining the various primary sources. What he felt obliged to conclude was that bribery, if it did occur, was only a very minor part of the narrative and that the key issues of borough compensation, patronage, and the Catholic question were far more decisive. The anti-corruption argument of Bolton proved convincing, and helped explain how certain practices, such as patronage, that might now seem unethical, were perfectly acceptable by the standards of the late-eighteenth century. The new orthodoxy held that the Union was an act of skilful management, and that while its passing might have challenged the boundaries of what was legal, it never actually crossed them.

Viscount Castlereagh – referred to the special funds as 'the means by which so much depends'.
(Linen Hall Library, Belfast)

The unearthing of a wealth of new archival material since the 1980s transformed previous interpretations about British activities in the 1790s. The majority of these papers concerned foreign policy, revealing the existence of a fully efficient intelligence organisation on the Continent that was, even then, being referred to in official documents as 'His majesty's secret service'. This revolution in historical evidence also applied to Ireland with the discovery of secret service papers that were previously 'missing'. Now available in the UK

William Pitt – when King George III recovered from illness in March 1801, Pitt had to persuade the king that he had indeed authorised covert funds. (National Gallery of Ireland)

National Archives, the documents reveal the existence of covert secret service activity in Ireland during the passing of the Union. In effect they constitute a second, secret set of secret service accounts, that were kept separate and distinct from the normal money that was accounted for legally, and which was catalogued in Gilbert. How these files went missing for almost two hundred years has never been adequately explained. What is clear is that a major cover-up was initiated after the passing of the Union to prevent any exposure of the illegal methods that had been approved. Documents and receipts were destroyed, fictitious accounts were approved, and the silence of those complicit in the activities was secured one way or another.

This paralleled directly the secret service money that was used on the Continent for espionage and counter-revolutionary activity. Technically the money was regulated and limited by various acts of parliament; in reality the legislation was wilfully ignored, and expenditure in the period made a mockery of the legal safeguards. According to Burke's civil list act (1782) for Britain, secret service expenditure had to remain within certain limits determined by parliament, usually £100,000. Ireland was governed by its own civil list act (1793) which suggested a figure of £5,000 for money used annually 'for detecting or preventing treasonable conspiracies'. In both domestic and foreign policy affairs these limits were ignored. A good example of the range of expenditure is that approximately £3,500 of secret service money was channelled into the conspiracy which culminated in the assassination of Tsar Paul I of Russia in 1801, while William Wickham's 'secret account' for funding counter-revolutionary activity on the Continent came to £3,682,520 for the first six months of 1800. It is in this context of European activity that the money sent to Ireland to assist the Union should be evaluated. In total the money came to £30,850, a significant but not a spectacular sum and the neo-corruption argument has concentrated largely on the possible use, or misuse, of this money. The chief secretary, Viscount Castlereagh, called the different sums 'the means by which so much depends', and one thing is certain about their purpose: the money was used for the creation of a covert slush fund, that could be used to respond to any exigency, and answer any emergency.

The Union that was passed successfully in 1800 was substantially different, in tone and content, from the one that had been embarrassingly rejected the previous year. For one thing its structure was significantly reworked, with the idea of appointing commissioners to negotiate it along the lines of the Scottish union of 1707 abandoned. While corruption, patronage and intimidation had not been lacking in January 1799, Dublin Castle, taking its lead from London, had been reluctant to countenance expensive gestures, and costly interventions were largely ignored. The greatest expenditure of all was not accepted: borough compensation. The parliamentary seats that were regarded as property were not to be treated as such, and proprietors were not to be compensated for their abolition, diminishing the attractiveness of the Union in the eyes of many owners. Catholics were also kept at arms length from the measure, with the government abandoning initial interest in Emancipation to appease the more powerful Protestant interests.

Forced to regroup and re-examine their options after their parliamentary defeat, the Castle took key decisions in 1799 that altered drastically the style and structure of the Union. The most important of these was the enthusiastic adoption of the 'three Cs' to secure victory: compensation, Catholic Emancipation and corruption. The union debate has largely centred on the final of these areas, but a strong case can be made for the significance of the first two. The figure for borough compensation was estimated in February 1799 at approximately one and a quarter million pounds, a total that provides another useful context for evaluating the secret service money. Hesitant MPs, like Edmund Burke's correspondent Sir Hercules Langrishe, received substantial compensation for the loss of their seats making the Union easier to contemplate. Although vigorous opponents of the measure, like the Marquess of Downshire, also received money for the abolition of their seats, because borough compensation had not been on offer in 1799 it soon became viewed as part of the general corruption on display. The new Catholic component of the Union scheme was kept more discreet. In November 1799 the cabinet in London informed the visiting Castlereagh that the lord lieutenant was authorised to promise Emancipation if the fate of the Union hung on the support of the Catholics. The viceroy, Cornwallis, had been a highly effective spin-doctor on behalf of the Catholics, and had made it clear that while their support could not ensure victory, their opposition would guarantee defeat. This was probably the case, and as the cabinet were terrified of seeing the Union rejected a second time they conceded the point. While theoretically the government could attempt the Union annually until it passed, in real terms they knew they had only one more chance. Perennial defeats would only reinforce the arguments of the opposition, and demonstrate that the ministry was determined to pass the measure whatever the wishes of the commons or the country.

Having secured the acquiescence, or at least neutrality, of the Catholic masses, and after having removed the most potent grievance of the proprietors, all that remained was to win friends for the measure and influence members. This is where the secret slush fund came into operation, keeping recalcitrant individuals content until an official, and legal, pension, could be secured for them by the granting of an office or sinecure. The fund was also to be used for the propaganda war, paying printers' bills, employing polemicists, and possibly even buying up opposition pamphlets so that they could be destroyed.

The money was paid in five instalments: £850 in October 1799, £10,000 in January 1800, £10,000 in February, £5,000 in April and a further £5,000 in May. When the commons resumed in January 1800 the Castle were confident in the strength of their numbers, and the divisions over the following months would reveal that they were correct in their assumptions. However the administration refused to become complacent, recognising that the real work was now keeping their supporters happy and preserving their majority. This was not an easy task, and required every inducement and incentive available, and if necessary the use of intimidation. Patronage, as Bolton so ably explained, was crucial, from the promise of peerages at the highest level to pensions and places at the lowest. This, of course, was part of the normal parliamentary traffic of the country, and although the Castle echoed Lord Harcourt's doomed administration in its liberality, it did not cross the line into illegality. Offering official rewards to government supporters was nothing new, and, although sometimes criticised, it was generally accepted as an integral part of the political game. Hard cash, on the other hand, was not.

Directing the transfer of funds from London was John King, ostensibly an under-secretary at the Home Office, but in reality the head of the Alien Office, a shadowy sub-department that ran 'His Majesty's secret service' on the Continent. It was King who liaised with Castlereagh, and who was always on hand whenever the Castle lost confidence. On 27 February 1800 the chief secretary admitted that there was little chance of converting opposition members as they were 'steady to each other'. But significantly, he revealed that if the slush fund went dry their support would haemorrhage. Even a few defections could be disastrous. The message was blunt: 'We require your assistance and you must be prepared to enable us to fulfil the expectations which it was impossible to avoid creating at the moment of difficulty. You may be sure we have rather erred on the side of moderation'.

The demands became more immoderate as the Union debates continued. With rumours of a similar opposition fund reaching £100,000 there was great unease as every resource of the administration was strained to breaking point. The requests became more frequent and more forceful, with Edward Cooke, the castle under-secretary for the civil department, informing King that further money was 'absolutely essential for our demands increase'. After every transaction Castlereagh sent a receipt for the money, promising to be 'fully accountable'. These receipts were kept separate from the other secret service accounts, with their existence known to only a handful.

The passing of the Union in June 1800 did not mark the end of the Castle's campaign; in many ways the following months proved more difficult as the ministers struggled to meet their pledges. Various financial debts had also accrued that needed acting upon, and further secret service money from England was not forthcoming. With the existing slush fund already exhausted, an ingenious method was hit upon to raise additional finance. The Castle discovered that a saving of £18,000 had been made on the Irish civil list in 1800. Instead of sending this money to the king, as required by law, Castlereagh received direct authorisation from London to channel the money into paying supporters of the

Union. This unorthodox procedure was sanctioned by the prime minister, Pitt, the home secretary, Portland, and even received the approval of King George III himself. In effect they were enabling the Castle to embezzle the necessary funds, to be replaced at a future, unspecified date. What this £18,000 was used for is not clear. Certainly the Castle had purchased seats that had fallen vacant, and had encouraged sympathetic figures to do the same, so these debts needed to be met. The propaganda war had also been won at a price, with printers now demanding that their debts be discharged. The Castle's unease about these claims is significant. With the spectre of exposure hanging over them, they were not prepared to risk their own reputations, and that of the Union, while victory was still being celebrated.

The collapse of the government in 1801 shattered their complacency. The fall of Pitt, on matters directly arising out of the passing of the Union, chiefly the Catholic question, saw a new ministry form under Henry Addington. In Ireland, Cornwallis and Castlereagh resigned in sympathy, and the Earl of Hardwicke prepared to take over as lord lieutenant. Events in England, however, had more unfortunate implications for the Union, as the king again succumbed to the mental and physical illness he had experienced in 1788-89. This delayed the transfer of ministerial power in London, with two cabinets existing side by side, and with one prime minister waiting to hand over his seals of office to the next. This confusion created many complications, and much embarrassment, such as the time when Addington and Pitt discovered they had both turned up for the same cabinet meeting. The king recovered in March 1801 but the problems did not end there. The change of ministry required a regulation of the finances, and suddenly accounts had to be produced and approved for all areas. This would not have been a problem, except that the king's memory had been affected by his illness and he now had no recollection of having authorised certain transactions. Upon discovering that £18,000 was missing from his privy purse, he immediately assumed that ministerial corruption was to blame. Suspecting the outgoing home secretary, Portland, of having embezzled the money, George III threatened to reveal everything, insisting he would not shield anyone who had been involved in 'corrupt measures in Ireland'. Exposure would have undermined fatally the legitimacy of the Union, providing evidence for the opposition's claims about the illegality of its passage. The crisis was, however, defused in the summer when Pitt intervened and persuaded the king that he had indeed authorised fully any covert Union activities. A fictitious set of accounts was prepared by the Home Office, and Portland was allowed to resign his office.

The change of administration in Ireland led to a shift in the political dynamic. With Cornwallis and Castlereagh gone, the only remaining figure who was aware of what had been done to secure the Union was Edward Cooke. Indeed it was for this reason, and no other, that Castlereagh had begged him not to resign with everyone else. The new viceroy, Hardwicke, however, was not briefed before he came to Ireland, and for a time suspected Cooke of having been involved in embezzlement. Mortified, Cooke reacted with genuine anger, and Hardwicke was forced to apologise. Nevertheless much bad feeling was created, and Cooke became an increasingly peripheral figure in the new Castle administration. His only real responsibility was fulfilling the Union promises, and to this end he wrote to John King at the Alien Office in October 1801 requesting £14,800 to meet pressing debts. Insisting that delay was 'dangerous and discreditable', his nervousness underlines the seriousness of what was at stake. In the end, the secret service fund could only supply a small sum, but the fact that £14,800 had already been spent on the Union campaign, and needed to be met, means that this figure should also be included in the total for Union corruption.

The new Union debate about corruption has almost exclusively concentrated on the secret service funds of £30,850. It is clear, however, that the £18,000 from the civil list and the £14,800 from autumn 1801 should also be added, making a final total of £63,650. Even this figure might not represent the complete amount, as money may have been channelled from other sources to help finance the covert Union campaign, and for which the details have never surfaced. For example, the misuse of Irish civil list money is only known because of the subsequent collapse of the ministry. In the cover-up which took place after the Union, almost all the evidence was destroyed that could allow the secret details of the transactions to be revealed. However, the documents that did survive allow for a reconstruction of some of the secret Union dealings, as well as for speculation about other possible activities of the Castle. And the fact that Irish MPs were still terrified in 1804 about their actions being revealed provides further evidence of the magnitude of the corrupt dealings that had taken place in Ireland in 1799-1801.

Undermined by the twin engines of patronage and intimidation, the defence of the Irish parliament crumbled in the first half of 1800. As the stalwarts of the opposition had been unwilling to enlist the support of Catholics, their attempts to raise a clamour outside of parliament foundered when they discovered the Castle's manoeuvres in that quarter had left them bereft of possible allies. Demoralised but defiant, the steadfast opponents of the Union debated to the end but the outcome was never in doubt. Why their opposition failed can not be attributed to any single reason. Many factors were at work, and much recent debate has centred on whether the Union was genuinely unpopular in the country. But, ultimately, everything was decided by the battle in parliament and there the anti-unionists proved ill-equipped and incapable of combating the various weapons and tactics of the Castle. Without doubt the most interesting element of the new Union debate is the recently discovered secret service papers. But the slush fund only assisted the government's campaign, and the key elements remained patronage, the Catholic question, borough compensation, but also the many valid and genuine arguments made in favour of union. Coming after the 1798 rebellion had discredited the Irish parliament in many eyes, these factors combined to reveal that the Irish polity was on its last legs in 1800: the cancer of corruption ensured that the illness was terminal.

Chapter Fifteen

The rising of 1803 in Dublin

Ruan O'Donnell

The rising of 1803 bore as much resemblance to what had been planned by its chief military strategist, Robert Emmet, as the rebellion of 1798 did to Lord Edward Fitzgerald's original plans. In both instances United Irish offensive activities had been envisaged as secondary to those of a sizeable French expeditionary force. Contingencies devised by the military committee of the United Irishmen between 1796 and 1803 were conceived as those appropriate for untrained and lightly equipped auxiliaries in support of a primary body of French professionals. The French were to supply officers, men, cavalry, artillery, munitions, firearms and their reputation for invincibility in the field. In short, the Parisian administration was expected to make good its offer to underwrite the Irish revolution. The assistance promised by the United Irishmen was to take the form of widespread and staggered diversionary actions to tie down British garrison personnel behind government lines. Victory would be effected by attacks on communications around the capital and the orderly mobilisation of insurgents in sectors where French cadres were accessible. By 19 May 1798 and 16 July 1803, however, the respective United Irish leaderships opted instead for the desperate gamble of a unilateral uprising ahead of any expected reinforcement from France. Both strategies faltered in Dublin, although the impressive degree of preparation attained in 1803 was not fully revealed owing to Emmet's decision to countermand orders to rise and the inability of State forces to confront the insurgents in their midst.

Similarities between the two projected conspiracies may be attributed to the common involvement of Philip Long, John Allen, William Dowdall, Walter Cox and several other important military committee associates. Emmet, although an officer in the St Stephen's Green division of the United Irishmen in May 1798, evidently only reached the inner circle of the organisation in August of that year. He rose still further to inherit Fitzgerald's crucial role in October 1802. By then the collapse of the Peace of Amiens in March 1802 seemed likely to bring a French invasion fleet to Irish shores on a scale not seen since December 1796. Prior to his reappearance in Dublin, Emmet had been personally assured

J.D. Reigh
1890

July 23, 1803.—ROBERT EMMET HEADS HIS MEN.

July 23, 1803. Robert Emmet heads his men by J. D. Reigh.

of French intentions, as he informed Miles Byrne, by Talleyrand and Napoleon Bonaparte. Emmet consulted widely with United Irishmen on the Continent, from Hamburg to Cadiz, in the summer of 1802, and on his return to Dublin in October was told that nineteen counties were prepared to rise en masse to aid the French.

Much attention was subsequently paid by Emmet, Long and Dowdall to city fighting although, as with so many other aspects of the planned coup d'état, little of this investment was visible on 23 July 1803. They realised, nonetheless, that the Irish executive at Dublin Castle was physically vulnerable and easily isolated from army headquarters at the Royal Hospital, Kilmainham. Moreover, the viceroy, Lord Hardwicke, lived outside the city in the Phoenix Park with a small staff of retainers and bodyguards. The chances of French progress in the provinces were obviously much greater if surprise attacks killed, captured or trapped the viceroy, privy council and commander-in-chief at the height of an invasion crisis. The prospect of wresting the Castle from state control would also have been a major morale boost for the United Irishmen expected to rally to the French en route to Dublin. The city, therefore, was the key to United Irish strategy, and the challenge of seizing control of it absorbed Emmet's coterie in the spring of 1803.

The conspirators hired an unknown number of premises in Dublin where war material was manufactured and stored. Walter Cox claimed knowledge of at least nine buildings where firearms were concealed, although the two most important known depots in Mass (a.k.a. Marshal) Lane South and Patrick Street contained very few. Buildings in North King Street, Smithfield, Winetavern Street, Capel Street, New Row and many other locations were employed for this purpose. Sophisticated ordnance such as rockets, mines and explosive devices ('infernals') were obtained in the south city. Robert Emmet's interest in the use of sophisticated ordnance perplexed many United Irish contemporaries, not least Wexford hero Thomas Cloney, who deemed them a waste of resources.

Cloney's point was debatable, but they were not, however, bizarre affectations of a misguided fanatic. The manufacture of hinged pikes was a simple and inexpensive means of giving urban revolutionaries an easily concealed weapon that was markedly superior to a sentry's bayonet. This initiative had been suggested by the problems encountered on the night of 23–24 May 1798, when mobilising United Irishmen, including perhaps Robert Emmet, were rendered all too obvious by their possession of eight-foot-long pikes. Military-grade black powder was available in small quantities from licensed dealers, and at least 140 pounds of cannon powder remained in the Marshal Lane South depot when discovered in the aftermath of the rising. Stocks of this explosive compound were used to prime signal rockets which Emmet had warned trusted associates

Lieutenant General Henry Fox by J. W. Chandler. As a result of the commander-in-chief's complacency, Emmet's insurgents were not opposed by any Crown forces acting under specific orders until after the rising petered out. (Public Record Office of Northern Ireland)

to watch for at 9 p.m. Rockets had been successfully test-fired at Irishtown and in the Dublin mountains above Rathfarnham in the spring of 1803, and those perfected by Emmet's staff were entirely serviceable. It has been suggested that British expert William Congreve adapted Emmet's designs for those he developed for the Royal Navy, but the salient fact is that the rockets were

Great Court Yard, Dublin Castle, by James Malton. The castle was the main object of Emmet's projected coup d'état. (National Library of Ireland)

effective. In fact, the launch of one rocket in Dublin city on 23 July 1803 warned the suburban rebel units to stand down; the sight of three would have signalled that the time had come to strike local objectives. Lord Edward Fitzgerald had envisaged using rockets in this role in May 1798, and it seems highly likely that his successor as chief military strategist, Emmet, was confirmed in his view of their utility by contact with the famous American engineer Robert Fulton whilst living in Paris in 1800–02. Other improvised explosive devices were crafted by Emmet's assistants in Marshal Lane South and Patrick Street, including the much-feared 'infernals'. Essentially, the infernals were bored and plugged logs packed with black powder and readied for detonation by fuses. Each log was rendered more lethal by hammering deal strips to their length that held small stones, metal scraps and nails in place. Emmet decided to bind two infernals to each other and mount them together on small carriages from which the wheels had been removed. Thus elevated, immobilised and sited in confined, narrow streets, the initial blast wave would have dispersed splinters, stone shards and jagged metal with terrible effect. Neither cavalry nor infantry were likely to hold formation if attacked by such a weapon, and seizing them prior to detonation would have been complicated by the necessity of approaching zones overlooked by rebel musket men and grenadiers.

It seems that the infernals were deployed in a defensive role and that Emmet lacked the finances to either prepare culvert mines or unleash multiple rockets against enemy positions. Nevertheless, it seems clear that Emmet was the first revolutionary to envisage widespread use of improvised explosive devices against garrison forces in Ireland. They were to be used during the critical mobilisation phase to drive the garrison off the streets and keep them corralled in their barracks. The military did not have to be annihilated-an unlikely prospect in any case-but it was imperative that their capacity to confront the popular forces was dealt a major blow in the initial stages of the revolt. Such breathing space, coupled with such variable factors as charismatic leadership and local military success, was the difference between attaining mobilisations of the contrasting levels seen in counties Wexford and Westmeath in 1798.

The British army itself was untrained in fighting in built-up areas and had never faced on home soil the improvised weapons envisaged by Emmet. All western military forces were obsessed with the practices of column advances and the ranks, files and squares that typified the formalised contests of the Napoleonic Wars. Neither cavalry nor artillery could be properly deployed in urban zones, and the extreme difficulty of organising and manoeuvring regulars in such conditions would have been exacerbated by the impediments of smoke once combat was joined. Furthermore, Emmet wished to fight at night and to prepare his chosen ground with spiked chains, fire and barricades to further limit the options of his enemies. The response of the soldiery to a deluge of grenades and musketry from elevated positions and their ability to maintain an efficient rate of fire when threatened by massed pikemen on all sides were open to question. Furthermore, several hundred easily concealed pistol calibre muskets had been commissioned by Emmet to give the insurgents a much better chance of prevailing against the 4000 regulars in Dublin. Miles Byrne procured in excess of 400 such weapons from gunsmith Daniel Muley, and James Hope obtained an unknown quantity of high-quality blunderbusses from another source. Daniel Muley's 1803 commission to produce 400 pistol calibre short muskets arose from the desirability of obtaining weapons suited to street fighting without alerting the watchful authorities.

This sudden onslaught in the city centre was to be seconded by an influx of thousands of rebels from counties Kildare, Wicklow and Meath, all of which were within walking distance of Dublin. Pike dumps were established for their use along the banks of the Royal Canal, in Rathcoffey (Kildare), Santry Woods (Dublin) and undoubtedly many other locations. Attacks on Belfast, Limerick and Cork, meanwhile, would increase pressure on the executive, which Emmet aimed to paralyse within the capital. The precise strategy of the Emmet group vis-à-vis the countryside was never divulged, let alone the last-minute contingencies adopted in haste after 16 July 1803, but such factors as staggered uprisings, ambushes and fighting columns were evidently considered. As before, market towns located on provincial road routes radiating from the capital would be occupied and defended. Dunshaughlin, Dunboyne, Lucan and similar outlying villages were earmarked for capture by men who had played the same role in the same places in May–June 1798. Each nodal point would contain the nucleus of a mobilising rebel column. The actual closure of roads by rebels in Celbridge, Maynooth, Phibsborough, Sandymount and Rathfarnham on the night of 23 July 1803 points to the viability of Emmet's plans and their considerable potential if triggered further afield. This was also emphasised by the unopposed march to the capital of insurgents from Straffan, Naas, Clane and other parts of County Kildare.

Most of the United Irish veterans in contact with Emmet's circle had undertaken to operate as auxiliaries alongside the French, or even without foreign assistance, if given modern weapons. They had sworn to perform this duty in 1797–98 and remained committed in the aftermath of defeat in the field to abide by their oaths in 1802–03. Failure to deliver either a French expeditionary force or the new muskets, therefore, fatally compromised the conspiracy. This dilemma arose owing to an accidental explosion in the rocket depot on Patrick Street on 16 July 1803 that forced the hand of the leadership. Darby Byrne and one Keenan were mortally wounded, and the frantic attempt to conceal the cause of the resultant fire led to conflict with the watchmen. Unbeknownst to Emmet, the military had refused to aid the watchmen that night without permission from a civilian magistrate, and the Castle authorities were powerless to arrest persons on suspicion owing to the revocation of coercion legislation in 1802. Byrne and Keenan spurned the inducements and threats of their captors and died within days under guard in Steevens's Hospital.

Fearing that all the crucial dumps would be discovered in house-to-house searches, Emmet sided with those who argued that an immediate uprising would oblige the French to expedite the invasion expected in August–September. A hastily convened conference in Windy Arbour (Milltown) on 16 July 1803 fixed the date of the uprising for 23 July. Given the sense of exigency, there was no provision for cancellation and insufficient time to acknowledge the responses of regional leaders. This meant that the outright opposition of most commanders to fighting with pikes alone was not appreciated in the capital until it was too late for Emmet to stand down his Leinster adherents. Communications with the Michael Dwyer faction in west Wicklow also proved less than ideal and broke down entirely when most required. Thomas Russell, James Hope, William Hamilton and other long-standing radicals went to Ulster to warn their contacts, while Dublin residents such as Miles Byrne and Arthur Devlin primed fellow Leinstermen. William Todd Jones and William Norris made overtures at the same time in Munster, and it seems that Limerick, if not also Cork, was originally intended to be attacked on 23 July. The reception of the delegates in most instances was far from positive given the magnitude of what was in train and it is highly likely that the rising would have been cancelled had Emmet realised that sufficient Ulster forces to capture Belfast, Downpatrick and Ballymena would not be fielded at the moment of truth.

The first attacks in Dublin were entrusted to squads of heavily armed men who gathered in private houses close to their objectives. Miles Byrne and William Darcy were primed in Denis Lambert Redmond's Wood Quay home for the attempt on the main Castle gates: another squad was simultaneously poised to break through the weakly defended Ship Street perimeter wall. Townsend Street rebels were tasked with raiding the ordnance store they lived beside, aided by their republican neighbours from Fleet and Poolbeg Streets. Ringsend and Irishtown rebels on the south coast were to strike at the Pigeon House Fort and a dump was maintained for their use by Thomas Brannigan. Smithfield area rebels in the north inner city were to tie down the substantial garrison of 2100 men based in the Royal Barracks (now the National Museum of Ireland at Collins Barracks) and hinder their efforts to cross the Liffey into the main rebel mobilisation area. The Liffey bridges would have been hotly contested. Patrick McCabe's men also reconnoitred outlying military installations on the north side with a view to storming the Phoenix Park Magazine and Islandbridge artillery barracks. Given the impracticality of holding such positions from garrison counterattack, it is likely that the magazine would have been burned and the cannon at Islandbridge spiked to prevent their use against the insurgents.

While the first wave exploited the element of surprise, Emmet, Dowdall, Allen and Long envisaged the rapid disbursement of pikes to the main reserve on Thomas Street near the focal point of the Corn Market building. At least 7,000 pikes were stored nearby in Marshal Lane South for the use of these men. The core group of 2,000 men from both County Dublin and the inner city was to have massed on Crumlin Commons and infiltrated Sylvester Costigan's Thomas Street distillery during the late afternoon. Armed in secret and behind chained doors, this cadre would have provided a backbone to the low-level activists told to mass in the pubs, groceries and dens of the south city ahead of further instructions. Hope had agitated amongst the Coombe United Irishmen towards this end, and the highly effective Colonel Felix Rourke of Rathcoole, a hero of the Leinster campaign in 1798, was destined to command. Other rebel officers were concealed in Thomas Court, College Green and two pubs operated by United Irishmen: the White Bull Inn and Yellow (a.k.a. 'Golden') Bottle on Thomas Street. The mere coalescence of such men severed the most direct route between

Dublin Castle and army headquarters at the Royal Hospital, Kilmainham, and, as such, it is not surprising that Emmet deployed chains, 'infernals' and sentries to protect the Liffeyside approaches to his primary body of manpower. Rebel officers also formed up with hand-picked men at Rainsford Street to guard the Canal Basin and the James's Street side of the critical zone. Rourke and his men shot at least two dispatch riders in the early evening and fired upon senior garrison officers en route to a conference in the Royal Hospital.

Emmet and his main associates spent much of the morning and early afternoon briefing subordinates in safe houses around the south city and soon realised that the situation regarding arms and the French was bound to cause dissension. Kildare men heard unfounded rumours that their Dublin comrades would not fight, and some leaders exerted themselves to send their followers home. The unexplained absence of Hope in Ulster evidently irritated many of his acquaintances in the Coombe who were not known to Rourke, let alone Emmet or Dowdall. When the truth about arms provision became apparent, a substantial element of Kildare forces withdrew from the city environs. Meanwhile, unauthorised attacks on army officers, magistrates, soldiers and loyalists threatened to alert the government in the early evening. Palmerstown magistrates Richard Willcocks and Edward Clarke were shot and wounded on Arran Quay when returning from the Castle. It was correctly assumed that they had reported their fears of an uprising, although Emmet had no way of appreciating the profound confusion within the executive at that time. Essentially, a republican riot was expected, not a full-blown attempt at insurrection, and while Lord Lieutenant Hardwicke and Under Secretart Alexander Marsden believed that the army would patrol after dark, commander-in-chief Lt-Gen Henry Edward Fox thought otherwise. Inexperience, incompetence and overconfidence disposed Fox to accept the misconception that the civilian yeomanry would shoulder the burden of security duties. The net result was that Emmet's insurgents were not opposed by any Crown forces acting under specific orders until after the rising petered out.

By 9.15 p.m. Emmet decided that the rising could not succeed and took steps to preserve the lives of his followers. The Mansion House on Dawson Street had been raided for arms and Henry Howley compromised the carriages needed for the rush on the Castle gates by shooting Colonel Lyde Brown during a fracas on Bridgefoot Street. Two small patrols of watchmen and magistrates had also been driven away from the Thomas Street vicinity by Rourke's sentries and men who had just been equipped with pikes at the Corn Market House. A protracted, bloody and doomed struggle seemed in the offing, which Emmet wished to avoid. Consequently, sizeable insurgent groups straddling the main suburban roads after 9.00 p.m. were stood down by the launching of a solitary signal rocket that countermanded orders to rise. Shortly afterwards Emmet emerged from the Thomas Street depot and hastily read extracts from a 'Proclamation of the provisional government to the people of Ireland'. He then headed a feint on the Castle in order to bring approximately 200 junior followers into the Dublin Mountains. The élite veteran groups such as that led by Byrne were not deployed when Emmet moved away from Thomas Street towards Rathfarnham. The chance encounter with and fatal piking of the Chief Justice. Lord Kilwarden, on his way towards the Castle had proved the final straw that exposed the limits of Emmet's control over those already on the streets.

Not considered by Emmet was the determination of several well-organised factions under recognised leaders to confront state forces. McCabe, Owen Kirwan, Peter Finnerty and Thomas Keogh were amongst the insurgent officers eager to fight at the head of separate corps. As Emmet approached Rathfarnham, at least 400 and probably many more insurgents fought a series of short skirmishes with two distinct elements of the 21st Regiment. The clashes moved from Thomas Street to the vicinity of the Coombe Barracks on Newmarket Street and scores of fatalities ensued. By 11.00 p.m. these efforts had resulted in the retreat of the military to barracks and the dispersal of their protagonists. Accordingly, the subsequent deluge of troops from Cork Street and Old Custom House Barracks found much evidence of an uprising but very few obvious participants. This exchange was by no means the fiasco the Castle, army and parliament were keen to project to a curious French gallery and to a British population living in fear of a cross-channel attack on their own shores.

Emmet and his main Kildare and Wicklow associates hid in the Ballynameece, Bohernabreena and Ballinascorney district of the Dublin mountains until 27 July, when he returned to his still-secret Harold's Cross lodgings to confer with surviving leadership figures in the city. The French were still expected within weeks if not months, and Miles Byrne was sent to Paris to brief the United Irish embassy on what had transpired. The French were not, however, in a position to mount an expedition at such short notice, although September was still in contemplation for the oft-postponed Irish invasion. It was not to be. On 25 August 1803 Emmet was taken prisoner in Harold's Cross by the indefatigable Town Major Henry Charles Sirr and brought to the Castle. Tried on 19 September and executed the following day on Thomas Street, the loss of Emmet precipitated the total collapse of the plot. Rourke, Redmond and Russell were the only other leaders of note executed by late October, by which time the workings of martial law ensured that the United Irishmen were no longer in a position to offer immediate coordinated assistance to the French. The origins, course and consequences of the rising of 1803 will be debated for years to come, but it is clearly unsatisfactory to treat the subject as an insignificant occurrence in the long history of Anglo-Irish hostilities.

Chapter Sixteen

The (show?) trial of Robert Emmet

Adrian Hardiman

On 19 September 1803 Robert Emmet was tried for high treason in Green Street courthouse, found guilty, and sentenced to be hung, drawn and quartered. He was executed the next day in Thomas Street. It is often thought that the case against Emmet was one of irresistible strength, so that, for example, the corruption of his leading defence counsel, although deplorable, made no difference. But contemporary records disprove this, both in terms of the evidence that was available and of the applicable law.

Emmet was condemned to death after what was essentially a show trial. His nominated counsel, John Philpot Curran, was compelled to withdraw under threat of having his daughter Sarah's liaison with Emmet exposed. His replacement, Leonard McNally, the leading radical lawyer of the day, was also a government spy who received a special supplement to his annual secret pension for betraying Emmet. His reports to the Castle, both before and after the trial, are extant. Emmet himself was prevented from making any defence by the threat of the exposure of Sarah Curran as the author of letters found in his possession which, the attorney-general had told him, implicated the writer in treason. By these means the government were able to produce at the trial, as Emmet's work, several highly incriminating documents even though their contemporary correspondence reveals that they could not prove authorship in accordance with law. Finally, Emmet was executed for the offence of high treason, contrary to the Treason Act, 1351 (the same act under which Roger Casement was executed in 1916). But the law of treason was dictated by the judge to the jury in a way radically different from the way in which it had been applied in England in a great state trial less than ten years previously, a way that made conviction a virtual certainty.

The government of Ireland, led by Philip Yorke, Lord Hardwicke, as lord lieutenant and William Wickham as his chief secretary, had been caught napping by the events of Emmet's rebellion on 23 July 1803. Only the total disorganisation of the rebels saved them from catastrophe. The London government were highly critical of Hardwicke, and his very survival was in

Supplement with   "THE SHAMROCK."   Christmas, 1892

THE TRIAL OF ROBERT EMMET, SEPTEMBER 19th, 1803.
"When my country takes her place among the nations of the earth, then, and not till then, let my epitaph be written."

The trial of Robert Emmet, September 19th, 1803 by J.D. Reigh.

part due to the fact that his brother, Charles Yorke, was home secretary. The correspondence between the brothers and their respective officials makes it quite clear that London expected dramatic and highly visible progress in stamping out rebellion. A large number of rebels had been captured in arms, and from late August the Irish government had one or more capital trials each day, followed (except in the case of two prisoners who were acquitted) by public executions the next day. But all of the prisoners were 'miserably poor', as Wickham himself said, and plainly not leaders. There was, from a government point of view, a crying need for a prominent, preferably Protestant, victim on whom the rebellion could be blamed.

Emmet, unlike the other state defendants, had escaped from Dublin after the failed rebellion. There was no hue and cry for him specifically: he had not been recognised as the gorgeously uniformed figure who read a proclamation and led a motley group on Thomas Street. He was captured in Harold's Cross on 26 August, and, although not immediately identified, it was plain to Major Sirr, the city's chief of police, that he was a person of consequence despite his youth. This was evident from a number of documents, including a letter to the government, found in the house where he was staying. Once identified as Robert Emmet, brother of Thomas Addis Emmet, the United Irish leader of 1798, who had himself been expelled from Trinity College in Lord Chancellor Clare's political cleansing of that year, his symbolic and political value became obvious.

John Philpot Curran, Emmet's nominated counsel, was compelled to withdraw under threat of having his daughter's liaison with Emmet exposed. (National Library of Ireland)

In the days after his arrest Emmet and the Castle authorities eyed each other warily. Each had a very serious problem. Dwarfing everything in Emmet's mind was the fact that on his arrest he had been in possession of unsigned letters from his inamorata, Sarah Curran. These are plainly love letters, though cryptically expressed in places: they also suggest a knowledge of Emmet's plans for a rebellion and contain bitter reproaches of those who by their 'barbarous

Leonard McNally, John Philpot Curran's replacement, was also a government spy. (National Library of Ireland)

desertion and want of unanimity' led to its failure. Sarah had repeatedly asked Emmet to burn the letters but he had not done so: this omission now tortured him and, according to McNally's later secret reports, he thought of nothing else. By an extraordinary irony, when the letters were read in Dublin Castle, the government did not interpret them as love letters, much less guess at the identity of their author. They believed that 'the language of a love intrigue had been assumed as a means of misleading the government' and that the letters were military communications in a cipher that had not been cracked. Emmet, on the other hand, assumed that Yorke and Wickham had identified Sarah as the author of the letters.

The government were immensely excited at the idea of portraying Emmet, an educated Protestant from a family with a revolutionary pedigree, as the linchpin of the rebellion. They were preoccupied, however, with their perception that there was so little hard evidence against him that he might well be acquitted if they put him on trial. On 28 August 1803 Wickham wrote to Yorke's private secretary and surveyed the evidence against Emmet in a very pessimistic fashion. He listed that evidence under seven headings, five of which were documentary, including the letter to the government and the original draft of the rebels' proclamation of a provisional government. The other two were circumstantial only. Wickham's problem was that Emmet's handwriting could not be proved: it could not be established that he was the author of the documents. He said that he had failed to find anyone who could 'say that they believed the papers of which we are in possession to be written by him ... we cannot, I fear, convict him without producing as his handwriting different papers written apparently by different persons', so that 'on account of the dissimilarity of the handwriting it would probably be thought more prudent not to produce them'. Worse, since Emmet 'was very much beloved in private life' he was pessimistic about getting other witnesses to testify as to Emmet's handwriting.

So pessimistic was Wickham that he contemplated a desperate measure, only to reject it:'The question of bringing forward secret information has been well considered and discussed, and there is but one opinion on the subject—viz., that it were a thousand times better that Emmet should escape than that we should close for ever a most accurate source of information.' In this letter Wickham is reporting not merely his own views but also those of the chancellor, Baron Redesdale, the attorney-general, Standish O'Grady, and the under-secretary, Alexander Marsden. It appears that they considered producing some agent who had for some time been 'a most accurate source of information' in a desperate attempt to convict Emmet. But they decided not to do so, even if it meant that Emmet would escape, because the source was so important. Dublin in the late eighteenth and early nineteenth centuries was full of spies and informers, so it is impossible to be sure who this person was. It is tempting in the circumstances, however, to speculate that it may have been Leonard McNally himself.

On 30 August Emmet was taken from Kilmainham jail to Dublin Castle for interrogation before the Irish privy council. He was refused the opportunity to consult a lawyer, so that he confronted the lord chancellor and the attorney-general—plus Wickham and Marsden—alone. The meeting was noted by Marsden in a surprisingly full way that brings out its drama. Emmet confirmed

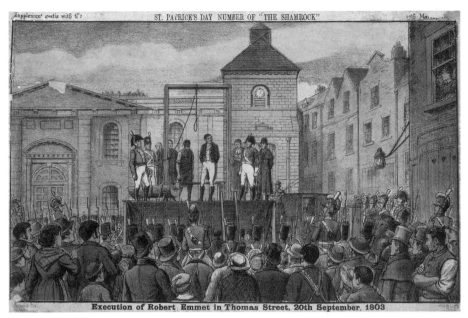

Robert Emmet on the scaffold outside St Catherine's Church, Thomas Street. (Kilmainham Gaol Museum)

his identity but otherwise refused to answer questions. This stand-off continued for a significant time until he was asked, 'By whom are the letters written that were found on your person?' Emmet replied, 'As to the letters taken out of my possession by Major Sirr, how can I avoid this being brought forward?'

This was the turning point of the interrogation, and indeed of the whole case against Emmet. He spoke freely and emotionally for the rest of the meeting and his interrogators spoke quite naturally too. Extraordinarily, although they noted that 'Mr Emmet's feelings are a good deal affected', the Castle men did not guess at the true cause of this.

The attorney-general told Emmet that the letters were important evidence against him and would have to be produced at the trial. They implicated him, and also the author of the letters, in treason. Emmet then imagined, it seems, that Sarah Curran had been arrested and asked anxiously whether 'anything has been done in consequence of those letters being taken'. He said that the author was a woman, and in a definitely pre-feminist attempt to exculpate Sarah he added, 'I can only say that a woman's sentiments are only opinions and they are not reality ... I declare on my honour that the person had only opinions'. Emmet attempted to appeal to contemporary sensibilities and concepts of honour, 'with notions of honour in common persons might have different principles but all might be agreed as to what a person might owe to a female'. But he got no assurances of any kind and eventually said 'I will go so far as this: if I have assurances that nothing has been done and nothing will be done upon those letters I will do everything consistent with honour to prevent their production … I would do anything to prevent the production of those letters'.

The meeting in the Castle ended inconclusively and Emmet was taken back to prison. On 8 September he was sufficiently distracted to write a letter to Sarah Curran under her own name and at her father's address in Rathfarnham. This he entrusted to a prison warden whom he thought was trustworthy: it was immediately placed in the hands of the authorities. Curran's house was raided by Major Sirr, though Sarah's sister seems to have been able to dispose of most incriminating documents. Sarah herself seems to have suffered a sudden nervous collapse. She was, however, treated very gently by the authorities. Her letters were regarded as curiosities and passed for the private perusal of the home secretary and the king himself. The former observed that 'Mademoiselle seems to be a true disciple of Mary Wollstonecraft'.

Once the interception of the letter to Sarah Curran became known to him, Emmet apparently thought of nothing but how to protect her. Thirty years later his junior counsel, Peter Burrowes (who was not in the pay of the Castle), told the poet Thomas Moore, a college friend of Emmet's, that he 'made the most earnest entreaties to the government that if they suppressed the letters at this trial he would not say a word in his own defence but go to his death in silence'.

There is no doubt that an arrangement was made between the government, who agreed not to identify Sarah, and Emmet, who agreed to mount no defence. This was probably done through Leonard McNally, who told the Castle three days before the trial that Emmet was wholly preoccupied with the risk to Sarah and was 'cruelly afflicted'. He 'does not intend to call a single witness, nor to trouble any witness for the Crown with a cross-examination, unless they misrepresent facts … He will not controvert the charge by calling a single witness'.

This, of course, was an extraordinary and absolutely corrupt letter for defence counsel to write to the prosecution before a trial. McNally was well paid for his treachery. He had, in any event, an annual pension from the government in respect of his work as an informer of £300 a year, which he drew from 1794 until his death in 1820. For his actions and omissions to act in Emmet's case he was paid a special bonus of £200. One hundred pounds of this was paid on 14 September 1803, five days before the trial: it is tempting to link this with his conveying an absolute assurance that the trial would be a walkover.

That an agreement was in fact made along those lines is demonstrated by two things in particular that happened in the course of the trial. The attorney-general in opening the case actually quoted from one of Sarah Curran's letters

Detail from Death coming for Lord Norbury. (Dúchas/Emmet family)

a passage in which she raised the question of whether French assistance was or was not desirable. This, however, he ascribed to 'a *brother* conspirator acquainted with his schemes and participating in his crimes'. He also quoted a passage suggesting that the Irish people were 'incapable of redress and unworthy of it', and that this accounted for the rebellion's failure.

The other revealing event occurred during the evidence of Major Sirr. He said that he had found certain letters on Emmet at the time of his arrest. The letters were produced and laid on the table of the court. Lord Norbury said, 'If the prisoner wishes to have any other part of these papers read [other than the part already read by the attorney-general] he may'. This appears to be a judicial intervention of the utmost fairness but its true significance is apparent from the response of Peter Burrowes, his uncompromised defence counsel: 'My Lord, the prisoner is aware of that, and throughout the trial will act under that knowledge'. Emmet was being reminded of what precisely his position was and that any attempt at defence would lead to Sarah Curran's exposure. Immediately afterwards, Burrowes attempted to address the jury but, according to what he later told Thomas Moore, Emmet stopped him from doing so, saying, 'Pray do not attempt to defend me—it is all in vain'.

Just before this intervention the attorney-general had attempted to get Sirr to read from a very incriminating letter to the government allegedly found in the room where Emmet had been arrested. No objection was taken but the court intervened, saying that 'nothing can be read but what is legally proved', an attitude that of course was embarrassing to the prosecution since they had no proof of handwriting. Extraordinarily, McNally declared that no objection was being taken to the admissibility of the letter. Norbury said that the court had wanted to protect Emmet from the admission of any evidence 'which is not strictly legal' but, having consulted with his colleagues after McNally's intervention, admitted it.

Any possibility that the attorney-general's misrepresentation of the gender of Emmet's correspondent might have been accidental is removed by a letter from the chief secretary to the British home office on the day of the trial: 'Mister Yorke [the home secretary] will have observed that the attorney-general when he gave in evidence such parts of the young lady's letter found upon Emmet as it was found necessary to produce, stated boldly that the letter from which the extract was made had been written by a *brother* conspirator [emphasis in original].'

One of the most obvious defects in the defence of Robert Emmet was the failure to even raise the question of whether his activities constituted treason as alleged in the indictment. Treason had always been a controversial charge because of its peculiar constitution in English law. It was the first common law offence to attain statutory definition, in 1351 under a statute of King Edward III. This, ironically, was introduced because the vagueness of the offence in common law made it an overly flexible political weapon. Accordingly, the indictment against Emmet charged treason in the classic form, that of 'compassing or imagining the death of the king'. This mental act *was* the offence: specific physical acts were merely the evidence of it. Over the centuries, there had been a tension between a narrow interpretation, requiring an actual intention *physically* to kill the king, and a broader approach that validated an offence of implied or 'constructive' treason, whereby an intention to depose the king was regarded as including an intent to kill him.

The 1790s were a decade of considerable radical activity in England as well as in Ireland. In 1794 there was a great state trial of leaders of the London Corresponding Society, a group favouring universal suffrage, annual parliaments and, it was alleged, the deposition of the king. In the trial for high treason of its leader, Thomas Hardy, and others, the prosecution and defence were conducted by two great luminaries of the English bar, Lord Eldon and Thomas Erskine. Eldon contended that it was sufficient if the persons charged intended 'to put the king in circumstances in which, according to the ordinary experiences of mankind, his life would be in danger'. Erskine contended for a literal construction of the act, requiring an intention physically to kill the king. He admitted that an intention to depose was something that entitled the jury to draw an inference that the prisoner intended to kill the king, but that was a matter for the jury and unless they did draw that inference Hardy could not be convicted of treason even though he had an intention to depose the king. Chief Justice James Eyre then left the issue of intention to kill to the jury. This was not done in Emmet's case, where the jury were simply told that if they accepted the evidence of the witnesses the offence of treason was complete. This deprived Emmet of the very point on which Hardy and his colleagues were acquitted.

Immediately following their acquittals, Pitt's government introduced an act, 36 George III, chapter VII, that extended the definition of treason from compassing the death of the king to any form of violence against the government, including conspiring with any foreigner to invade any part of the king's dominions. This would certainly have captured Emmet's actions as we know them. But this act did not apply in Ireland.

In the Irish state trials between 1798 and 1803 a much broader definition of treason than that available under English common law was used. Specifically the question of intent to kill the king was regarded by the judges as conclusively established by proof of an act of rebellion or an intention to depose, and was never left to the jury. According to Sir James Fitzjames Stephens's 1883 *History of the Common Law*, 'the doctrine against which Erskine is supposed to have prevailed in the trials of 1794 was applied to many later cases without hesitation. This occurred in the trials for the Irish Rebellion in 1798 and in particular of the two brothers Henry and John Sheares'. That is the very point: the cases in which the English decision of 1794 was ignored were all Irish cases.

The statute of 1795 also required that the overt acts of treason be proved by not less than two witnesses. In the case against the Sheares brothers there was only one relevant witness, the notorious felon-setter Captain Armstrong. When this point was taken by Curran on their behalf, the Irish court held that the requirement for two witnesses arose by statute only and in England only and not in Ireland, i.e. that the act of 1795 did not apply here. Fifty years later, when the Treason Felony Act of 1848 was introduced after the rebellion of that year, it recited that 'doubts were entertained whether the provisions (of the said 1795 Act) extended to Ireland': this is an understatement since it is perfectly clear from the decision of Lord Carleton in the Sheares case that the act did not apply here.

It should also be noted that there was an additional difficulty in contending for an implied intention to kill the king based on an act of rebellion in Ireland. King George III had never resided in or even visited Ireland. In the English state trials Lord Eldon had contended that deposing the king endangered his life 'according to the ordinary experiences of mankind'. This is much harder to maintain if the overt acts of rebellion take place on a different island. But this point, too, was ignored.

Although it might be said that Emmet would very likely have been convicted even if he had been defended by honest and competent counsel and allowed to make whatever defence he wished, and to cross-examine the witnesses, I think it is too easy to jump to this conclusion. The Crown did not go to the lengths described in this article for any reason other than fear that their case might collapse. Two of the trials in September 1803 ended in acquittal after a vigorous defence and thorough cross-examination, and Wickham himself feared that Emmet would be acquitted. As it was, the Crown was guaranteed its moment of glory as the leader of the rebellion went to the scaffold; McNally got his money, Sarah Curran her immunity and Emmet his martyrdom. As a bonus, the Crown also got John Philpott Curran: a month later, contemplating another legal difficulty, the Castle consoled itself that 'Mr Curran is completely in our power'.

Chapter Seventeen

Robert Emmet: Between memory and history

Kevin Whelan

A common observation about Robert Emmet is that he had a death-wish, that he was in thrall to blood sacrifice and the martyrdom complex. That misunderstands the nature of his ethical dilemma. There is a clear distinction between being a martyr and being a suicide. Suicide you choose: martyrdom has to be inflicted on you by someone else. Martyrdom is always achieved posthumously. Emmet did not wish to die. He saw himself as a serious revolutionary whose function was to be successful. At the same time, he had to be aware that if his project failed there were inevitable consequences. That does not mean that he was courting those consequences. In Emmet's case, his dignity and his tragedy derive precisely from the fact that he had the philosophical resources to know that he was facing an ethical dilemma. He walked this fine ethical line between knowing that his death was coming, embracing it and not embracing it. He did not choose to be hanged, then beheaded, and finally to have his gory locks held up to the admiring or disapproving Dublin multitude. But he realised that there is a burden with leadership: if you are not willing to suffer the consequences of your acts, are you then being morally or ethically irresponsible? At the same time there is a further temporal dimension: while you suffer a physical death at this precise moment, you may generate a living memory that keeps you perpetually alive, in suspended animation between history and memory. Emmet's last days occupied this charged and complex space between death, martyrdom and suicide. After the sentence of death was passed, he was removed back to Kilmainham with his legs in irons: he drew 'an admirable likeness of himself, the head severed from the body, which lay near it, surrounded by the scaffold, the axe, and all the frightful paraphernalia of high treason execution'.

Emmet understood that there were two types of death: the physical one of the body but also death by forgetting. The French philosopher Paul Ricoeur aphorises about the victims of political injustice that to be forgotten is to die again. For Emmet it was crucial that he should not be forgotten, and his famous speech was his defence against oblivion. Emmet ensured that his death was steeped in resonances of classical republicanism—the Senecan tradition of the death that puts the political and juridical system itself on trial. In his last letter to his brother on 20 September, he observed: 'I am just going to do my last duty to my country. It can be done as well on the scaffold as on the field [of battle].' His speech aimed 'to unmanacle his reputation' (his hands were manacled throughout his speech): he positioned it as 'a claim on your memory'. 'This is my hope, that my memory and name may serve to animate those who survive me.' The future would vindicate the principles for which he died.

As Seamus Deane has noted, a crucial feature of the speech is its use of the future perfect tense—the open-ended tense of nationalism. We can contrast the different tenses of nationalism and unionism: unionism preferred the past tense, spooling backwards relentlessly from 1798 to 1690 and 1641. Nationalism promulgated the future tense, scrolling forward through the teleology of 1798, 1848, 1867, 1916, 1969, to that future day when the nation would finally have come into being. This is the tense of Emmet's peroration, a carefully crafted piece of oratory pitched not to the contemporary moment but to an ever-unfolding future, and to those who would complete and perfect his republican vision.

That appeal to the future is what sent Emmet cascading down the echo chamber of Irish history. These words resonate not as words delivered from the dead past but from the living present, words that are a constant calling to conscience and judgement about the republic and where it stands now. The extraordinary resonance of the speech stems from the fact that it is not directed at the specific audience to which it was delivered. It is a speech that goes out over the dock and into the general populace. Its claim is that my ethics, my morals, my political principles are superior to those by which I am being judged. It is a Senecan speech that claims vindication in terms of superior ethics—my ethics are superior to the ethics of those who will judge me, who will condemn me to death and kill me. Emmet's peroration is projected into an ideal, a virtual future in which the republic will eventually have been achieved. It is only when the republic will finally have achieved constitutional embodiment that his legacy will have come into its own: only then can his epitaph be written. The speech—and Emmet's life—awaits the verdict of history for vindication, to give it meaning and closure. Because of that pitch, the speech is always contemporary.

Emmet understood, too, the power of the image. Shortly after 1 o'clock on 20 September 1803, he was executed publicly in front of St Catherine's Church, Thomas Street, Dublin. Emmet wore a plain black coat, black velvet stock, and Hessian boots, which gave him the classic appearance of the gentleman revolutionary. At his execution he was described as 'perfectly devout and composed'. As he was forbidden to address the crowd, once he arrived at the top

Irish Chief Secretary William Wickham: 'Had I been an Irishman, I should most unquestionably have joined him'. (Dúchas/Emmet family)

of the platform he simply said: 'My friends, I die in peace and with sentiments of universal love and kindness towards all men'. He then gave his watch to the executioner, Thomas Galvin, who bound his hands (lightly at Emmet's request) and drew a black hood down over his face. His body was taken down after hanging for thirty minutes (he died slowly because of his light frame). Because he was convicted of high treason, the hangman then clumsily severed his head with a large blade on a deal block from a local butcher. Grasping it by the hair, he held it high above the crowd, shouting: 'This is the head of a traitor, Robert

Emmet'. According to a young eyewitness, the 'people groaned in horror and anguish'. His blood seeped into the gutter and was lapped up by dogs. The severed head and body were brought back to Kilmainham Gaol 'and left for some time in the court of the prison where the prisoners might view it from their cells'. The bloody block was displayed for two days at Thomas Street. His staunchness ensured that he was rapidly elevated into the republican pantheon. Thomas Russell claimed that 'There were as many tears shedding for Emmet as would bathe him and that he would be considered by the people as a martyr'.

The crucial difference between the 1803 and 1798 insurrections was that the Act of Union had taken place in the interim. That of 1798 was a rebellion against an Irish government in College Green, whereas that of 1803 was directed against a British administration in the brand-new United Kingdom of Great Britain and Ireland. From the British perspective, the Union was designed to solve the Irish problem. In the characteristic British way, the principal architects of the Union (Pitt, Cornwallis) believed that the problem in the 1790s had emerged because the Irish, both Protestant and Catholic, could not rule themselves: once you inserted an impartial, imperial parliament into their internecine squabbles then the Irish would bed down under the Union just as the unruly Scots had done after their union in 1707. The cowed Irish would follow the Scots into docile, complacent and successful absorption into the Union. Emmet's rebellion against a British administration ('Our object was to effect a separation from England') so soon after the passing of the Union made it crucially different to 1798. Emmet had earlier stressed to the French that seeming Irish placidity when the Union was passed was only 'the silence of politics, under a state of persecution'. In 1803 he argued that Britain had taken 'even the name of independence from Ireland, through the intervention of a parliament notoriously bribed, and not representing the will of the people'. It was the challenge to this union that sent the shock waves reverberating through Dublin Castle and the London establishment: the insurrection indicated that the Irish problem was not going to be resolved by the Act of Union but might actually intensify. Castlereagh was infuriated by it because he 'could not see the change that his own great measure the Union has effected in Ireland'. The fact that it was a military catastrophe did not matter: once again, you had Irish insurrection; once again, armed rebels stalked the Dublin streets; once again, there was the threat of a French invasion; once again, insurrection was not instigated by the usual suspects, the disgruntled papists, but by this talented and intelligent young man who came from ascendancy Protestant privilege. The 1803 rising signalled that the Act of Union, rather than resolving Irish problems, was going to deepen them. That is why Emmet resonated so much across the nineteenth century. As long as the Act of Union was in place, the challenge to it so early in its life posed a pivotal question for both Irish nationalism and British unionism.

'Heroines of Irish history V: the torture of Anne Devlin'. The powerful triangulation around Emmet, Curran and Devlin provided a gender- and class-based model of Irish masculinity and femininity which had very little to do with the historical figures themselves. (Irish Fireside, 5 August 1885)

Emmet posed a 'spin' problem to Protestant commentators like Richard Musgrave, who did not—and, in a sense, could not—write about 1803. Because he was a Protestant drawn from the heart of the Dublin liberal establishment, literally born with a silver spoon in his mouth, Emmet gave the lie to the idea that sedition was a Catholic thing: 'We fight that all of us may have our country and that done each of us shall have his religion'. 'We war not against property—We war against no religious sect—We war not against past opinions or prejudices—We war against English dominion.' Thus Emmet made it impossible to repeat the massively successful Musgrave take on 1798 as a recrudescence of Catholic barbarity along the lines of the 1641 Rebellion. Secondly, 1803 was also a complete disaster for Dublin Castle, whose shambolic performance included a catastrophic breakdown of intelligence. There were two spectacular military failures in 1803: Emmet's and Dublin Castle's. Fox was a complete disaster as commander-in-chief. The fact that two key leaders—William Dowdall and John Allen—escaped encouraged Dublin Castle to pin all the blame on Emmet. They did not want Westminster to know that a wide-ranging United Irish conspiracy had been hatched under their very noses. Castlereagh advised them that 'the best thing would be to go into no detail whatever upon the case, to keep the subject clearly standing on its own narrow base of a contemptible insurrection without means or respectable leaders'.

Prior to his execution, Emmet wrote a letter to William Wickham from Kilmainham, thanking him for the fair treatment that he had received. Wickham received it hours after Emmet's death and was profoundly moved, not least by the fact that Emmet's very last letter was written 'in a strong firm hand without blot, correction or erasure'. Combined with Emmet's dying demeanour, it provoked an overwhelming change of heart in Wickham, causing him to doubt the legitimacy of British rule in Ireland. Until his death, Wickham remained haunted by the ghost of Emmet. He was spooked by this message from the grave, which he showed to all and sundry: 'For the long space of thirty-two years, it has been my constant companion'. He resigned in 1804 because he could no longer implement laws that were 'unjust, oppressive and unchristian' or bear the intolerable memory that he had been 'compelled by the duty of my office to pursue to the death such men as Emmet and Russell'. Of Emmet, he said: 'Had I been an Irishman, I should most unquestionably have joined him'. He was haunted by Emmet and the Gospel passage Matthew 6: 44–5: 'in what honours or other earthly advantage could I find compensation for what I must suffer were I again compelled by my official duty to prosecute to death men capable of acting as Emmet has done in his last moments, for making an effort to liberate their country from grievances the existence of many of which none can deny, which I myself have acknowledged to be unjust, oppressive and unchristian'.

As Wickham's experience demonstrated, Emmet had a huge impact on contemporaries. To many, he appeared to be an ethically admirable leader who sought to minimise bloodshed. The poet Robert Southey had visited Dublin

A member of the Irish National Foresters in Dublin, c. 1914, wearing a uniform inspired by depictions of Emmet. (Hulton Getty Picture Collection)

in 1801 and met Emmet's friend Richard Curran, brother of Sarah. On 28 September 1803 he wrote: 'If the government want to extirpate disaffection in Ireland by the gallows, they must sow the whole island with hemp'. Shelley visited Dublin in 1812, inspired by Emmet, and also wrote poems on him. Samuel Taylor Coleridge wrote on 1 October 1803: 'Like him, I was very young, very enthusiastic, distinguished by talents and acquirements and a sort of turbid eloquence: like him, I was a zealous partisan of Christianity and a despiser and abhorrer of French philosophy and French morals: like him, I would have given my body to be burnt inch by inch rather than that a French army should have insulted my native land.' In his notebooks Coleridge made the cryptic comment: 'Emmet = mad Raphael painting ideals of beauty on the walls of a cell with human excrement'. It is difficult not to conclude that Emmet was the accusing ghost for a generation of English Romantics (Wordsworth, Coleridge, Southey, etc.) swinging round from radicalism into conservatism.

Emmet was also portrayed in the nineteenth century as the ideal of Irish masculinity, the Irish Washington with his tight-fitting trousers, fine uniform and dashing air. He is shown as a prototype of what Irish masculinity should be. His rounded leg is determinedly thrust into the foreground: his beautiful, almost sexualised body is displayed in highly elaborate uniforms. Irish masculinity was emasculated through the nineteenth century, in the political and military spheres. Irish people were literally broken-backed, pock-marked, limping: the Irish body had become perforated, shrunken, tubercular, rheumatic—paralytic, in James Joyce's famous phrase. The whole corpus of nineteenth-century Irish literature hardly contains a single strong masculine figure. Portraying Emmet in this way made him an icon for Irish masculinity.

That representation was also worked into the nineteenth-century representation of his triangular relationship with Sarah Curran and Anne Devlin, which addressed the issue of appropriate role models for Irish women. Sarah Curran functioned as the model for the Protestant gentry woman: she should be etherealised, disembodied, sublimated and desexualised. Curran was permitted the flourishes of the romantic exile in Sicily and the high romantic sense of unrequited love brutally interrupted by an external force. Anne Devlin appeared as the Catholic peasant woman who is faithful, ministering to bodily needs, a servant who is endlessly loyal. She functions as the ideal of Irish maternal femininity in the nineteenth century—long-suffering, long silent, but always standing by her man. This powerful triangulation around Emmet, Curran and Devlin provided a gender- and class-based model of Irish masculinity and femininity which has very little to do with the historical figures themselves.

Emmet's speech was always used to calibrate the republican project in Ireland. Through the two centuries since 1803, those who have contemplated the health of the body politic have been drawn to Emmet's speech to answer the question: how is Ireland and where does she stand, how stands the republic now? These are difficult and fundamental issues: the ghost of Emmet reappears, particularly at moments of political redefinition. As long as the Union lasted, Emmet was a lively poltergeist in the political system. His rebellion occurred against a backdrop of the Act of Union, and as long as the Union was in place, the challenge to it was also in place: Emmet became shorthand for the refusal to accept that the Union was a definitive or just settlement of the Irish political situation. He appeared in an almost physical form in 1848 when Robert Holmes, his brother-in-law, was the lawyer who defended the Young Irelander John Mitchel prior to his transportation to Australia. A direct family link with Emmet has been deliberately drawn on. He re-emerged in the Fenian period in both its American and in its Irish phases: the Fenians themselves emerged out of the Emmet Monument Associations that sprang up in America in the 1850s. The 1903 Emmet centenary was a significant event, just as the 1798 centenary had been. The Irish nationalist tradition had become fractured and fractious over the issue of Charles Stewart Parnell's continued leadership of the Home Rule movement, which was poisonous to Irish nationalist self-confidence and which divided them for ten years. The 1798 and 1803 commemorations allowed them to share a platform, however acrimoniously, again. The republican project accelerated after 1903 in the wake of a huge Emmet commemoration when perhaps 80,000 marched in the streets of Dublin. It is no surprise that Emmet was powerfully present in 1916. Patrick Pearse engaged with the Emmet legacy. He eulogised Emmet as having 'redeemed Ireland from acquiescence in the Union. His attempt was not a failure but a triumph for that deathless thing we call Irish nationality.' One of the reasons he moved his pioneering school St Enda's up to the Hermitage in Rathfarnham in 1910 was precisely because of its Emmet association: he knew that he was literally walking in the footsteps of Emmet and Sarah Curran. When Pearse read his proclamation from the steps of the GPO, he was also self-consciously following in the footsteps of Emmet. Pearse had this enormous sense of a legacy from the past that needed to be vindicated. The last pamphlet that Pearse wrote before 1916 is entitled 'Ghosts. The most powerful of these ghosts is Emmet. When Pearse entered the GPO, it was not Cuchulain but Emmet that was at his shoulder.

Flying into Sydney, one flies over the white crescent of Bondi Beach, the famous surfing mecca. If you look at the clifftop overlooking it, you can see Waverly cemetery. The biggest 1798 monument in the world is located there, so big that it can actually be seen from the plane as you descend into Sydney. The memorial has chiselled onto it the roll-call of Irish republicans (because Irish republicanism is critical to the birth of Australian republicanism). Beginning with William Orr in 1797, it lists the United men, Tone, McCracken and Dwyer; then the Young Irelanders and the Fenians; then the 1916 leaders; the hunger strikers from the Northern Ireland Troubles have been added. But there is a parenthesis on that monument, two brackets that come in the sequence where Emmet's name should obviously appear. His name has not been chiselled onto the monument. Emmet's presence endures as an absence, a sense, perhaps, that Ireland has not fully achieved what it set out to achieve.

Bibliography

Bartlett, Thomas, *The Fall and Rise of the Irish Nation: The Catholic Question, 1690-1830* (Dublin 1992).

Bartlett, Thomas, David Dickson, Dáire Keogh and Kevin Whelan (eds), *1798: A Bicentenary Perspective* (Dublin, 2003).

Bartlett, Thomas, *Revolutionary Dublin, 1795-1801: The Letters of Francis Higgins to Dublin Castle* (Dublin, 2004).

Beiner, Guy, *Remembering the Year of the French: Irish Folk History and Social Memory* (Madison, 2007).

Blackstock, Allan, *An Ascendancy Army: The Irish Yeomanry, 1796-1834* (Dublin, 1998).

Cullen, L.M, 'The 1798 Rebellion in Wexford: United Irishmen organisation, membership, leadership', in Kevin Whelan (ed.), *Wexford: History and Society* (Dublin, 1988), 248–95.

Curtin, Nancy, *The United Irishmen: Popular Politics in Ulster and Dublin, 1791-1798* (Oxford, 1994).

Dickson, David, Daire Keogh and Kevin Whelan (eds.), *The United Irishmen: Republicanism, Radicalism and Rebellion* (Dublin, 1993).

Dickson, David, *New Foundations: Ireland 1660-1800* 2nd ed. (Dublin, 2000)

Dunne, Tom, *Rebellions: Memoir, Memory and 1798* 2nd ed. (Dublin, 2010).

Elliott, Marianne, *Partners in Revolution: The United Irishmen and France* (New Haven and London, 1982).

Elliott, Marianne, *Wolfe Tone: Prophet of Irish Independence* (2nd ed., Liverpool, 2012).

The Formation of the Orange Order 1795-1798: The Edited Papers of Colonel William Blacker and Colonel Robert H. Wallace (Belfast, 1994).

Furlong, Nicholas, *Father John Murphy of Boolavogue 1753-1798* (Dublin 1991).

Gahan, Daniel, *The People's Rising: Wexford 1798* (Dublin, 1995).

Geoghegan, Patrick M., *The Irish Act of Union* (Dublin, 1999).

Geoghegan, Patrick M., *Robert Emmet: A Life* (Dublin, 2002).

Keogh, Daire, *The French Disease: The Catholic Church and radicalism in Ireland, 1790–1800* (Dublin, 1993).

Keogh, Daire, *A Patriot Priest: The Life of the Revd. James Coigley, 1761-1798* (Cork 1998).

Kleinman, Sylvie, 'Ambassador incognito and accidental tourist: Cultural perspectives on Theobald Wolfe Tone's mission to France, 1796-8', *Journal of Irish and Scottish Studies* 2:1 (2008), 101-122.

McBride, Ian, *Scripture Politics: Ulster Presbyterians and Irish Radicalism in Late Eighteenth-Century Ireland* (Oxford, 1998).

Miller, D.W., (ed.), *Peep O' Day Boys and Defenders: Selected Documents on the County Armagh Disturbances 1784-1796* (Belfast, 1990).

Moody, T.W., R.B. McDowell, and C.J. Woods (eds), *The Writings of Theobald Wolfe Tone* (3 vols, Oxford, 1998-2007).

Murphy, John A, (ed.), *The French are in the Bay: The Expedition to Bantry Bay, 1796* (Cork, 1997).

O'Donnell, Ruán, *The Rebellion in Wicklow, 1798* (Dublin, 1998).

O'Donnell, Ruán, *Aftermath: Post-Rebellion Insurgency in Wicklow, 1799-1803* (Dublin, 2000).

O'Donnell, Ruán, *Robert Emmet and the Rebellion of 1798* (Dublin, 2003)

O'Donnell, Ruán, *Robert Emmet and the Rising of 1803* (Dublin, 2003).

Pakenham, Thomas, *The Year of Liberty: The Great Irish Rebellion of 1798* (London, 1969).

Patterson, James G., *In the Wake of the Great Rebellion: Republicanisn, Agrarianism and Banditry in Ireland after 1798* (Manchester, 2008).

Quinn, James, *Soul on Fire: A Life of Thomas Russell* (Dublin, 2002).

Senior, Hereward, *Orangeism in Ireland and Britain, 1795-1836* (London and Toronto, 1966).

Smyth, Jim, *The Men of No Property: Irish Radicals and Popular Politics in the Late Eighteenth Century* (Basingstoke, 1992).

Stewart, A.T.Q., *The Summer Soldiers: The 1798 Rebellion in Antrim and Down* (Belfast, 1996).

Whelan, Kevin, *The Tree of Liberty: Radicalism, Catholicism, and the Construction of Irish Identity, 1760-1830* (Cork, 1996).

Woods, C.J. (ed.), *Journals and Memoirs of Thomas Russell, 1791-95* (Dublin, 1991).